A PURITY OF ARMS

A PURITY OF ARMS

AN AMERICAN IN THE ISRAELI ARMY

AARON WOLF

Doubleday

NEW YORK   LONDON   TORONTO   SYDNEY   AUCKLAND

PUBLISHED BY DOUBLEDAY

a division of Bantam Doubleday Dell Publishing Group, Inc.
666 Fifth Avenue, New York, New York 10103

DOUBLEDAY and the portrayal of an anchor with a dolphin are trademarks of Doubleday, a division of Bantam Doubleday Dell Publishing Group, Inc.

"Those Were the Days," words and music by Gene Raskin, TRO. © Copyright 1962 and 1968 Essex Music, Inc., New York, N.Y. Used by permission.
"Hamilchama Ha'Achrona" written by Haim Hefer. © All rights reserved by the author, Israel. Used by permission.
"Here Comes the Sun" by George Harrison. © 1969 Harrisongs Ltd. Lyrics reproduced with kind permission from Harrisongs Ltd.
"Summertime" by George Gershwin and Dubose Heyward. © 1935 Chappell & Co. (Renewed). Used by permission. All rights reserved.
"Nirkod Nishkach" written by Shlomo Artzi. © All rights reserved by the author, Israel. Used by permission.
All photos copyright Aaron Wolf, unless otherwise noted.

Library of Congress Cataloging-in-Publication Data

Wolf, Aaron.
    A purity of arms : an American in the Israeli army / by Aaron Wolf. — 1st ed.
       p.   cm.
    1. Wolf, Aaron.   2. Jews, American—Israel—Biography.
3. Israel—Armed Forces—Military life.   I. Title.
DS113.8.A4W65   1989
956.94′004924073—dc20   89-35373
[B]   CIP

ISBN 0-385-26036-9

TO MY PARENTS, DEBORAH AND LEONARD,
FOR *THE PASSION OF ISRAEL*
AND A WHOLE LOT MORE.

ACKNOWLEDGMENTS

I am indebted to a number of people for their help with this book:

Daniel Goleman, who started the ball rolling; Fay Goleman for saving a space on her bookself; and Jamie Goldstein for keeping me honest. Thanks are due to Sadja Greenwood and Alan Margolis for taking in a stray student.

For helping me keep the facts straight, I want to thank James Schuler at the U.S. Department of State, John Miles of UNRWA, and particularly Colonel Ya'akov Itzhaki at the Israeli Consulate in New York. Sam Katz was helpful both in person and through his books.

I want to thank several people who gave their help and support when it was all happening: Cindy Alkon, Eric Kaufman and Debby, Shem-Tov, and Aram Hava, who opened their doors to me, and Claire Elbaz for accepting my collect calls. I am indebted to Kibbutz Kfar Hamaccabi for adopting me, and I owe special thanks to the Konnellos for making me part of their family.

And to Ariella, who was always there beside me, my love. Thanks, too, to her family for their support.

I want to salute the men and women of the Israel Defense Force, who, given the hardest work imaginable, do the best job possible.

Thanks also to Judy Sandman for her editing expertise and her patience.

Finally, this book would not be in its present form without the textual guidance of my father, the best tinsmith around.

Of course, all mistakes or oversights are my own.

NOTE

Everything described in this book happened. For reasons of security and privacy, almost all the names have been changed. But the events, the letters, and the feelings are real.

Madison, Wisconsin, September 1988

The coffee is real. So is the cream.

From my desk in our fifth-floor apartment I can look out the window and see the signs of my first Midwestern autumn. The oaks on the edge of Lake Mendota are beginning to turn and their leaves are falling. The sky and its reflection on the lake turn dark earlier with every evening. Last night we had our first snow flurries.

I'm back in the United States to be a graduate student. Ariella is with me.

On the way here, in California, we camped in the high Sierras. How vast they are! Enormous rock structures, boundless forests. Even the sky seems bigger. Horizon everywhere you look and not a border in sight. In Israel, there is no "away from it all."

Now, here we are, in Madison, and in culture shock. I've gone through it before and I know I'll get over it in time. Soon, I'll find out how Spider-Man has been doing and whatever happened to the U.S. Football League, and who Spuds Mackenzie is. Already I know that red M & M's are back.

Ariella, who has never lived here, has important questions. "Aharon," she asks, looking up from a magazine, "what is a Yuppie?"

We buy a TV set from Walmart. A couple of days later, she burst into the next room. "Aharon! You should have seen! I turned on the TV and this man had a brand-new car on the stage. Then a woman came running up. She guessed the price of the car and he gave it to her. He just gave it to her!"

Slowly, I fall into my new routine. Slowly, the parts of my brain that dealt with the rifle-fired grenade's capacity to penetrate steel focuses on the average hydraulic conductivities of various sediments and rocks.

I stop jumping when I hear loud noises.

I stop looking around for my rifle whenever I get up from a chair.

1

Lebanon, June 1987

This is the forty-second hour and I'm still awake. We've cleared the road five miles in one direction and now we're clearing it on the way back. We're moving in a T-formation. The guys on the flanks are checking for wires, booby traps, or mines. At the far right is David, lugging his heavy FN MAG machine gun. His eyes move from side to side, keeping time with the motion of the 7.62-millimeter barrel of his gun. The company commander, Ehud, is in the middle of the T. As his radio man, I'm right behind him, and the rest of the patrol is behind me, on the road itself, scanning the hillsides, checking the terraces for moving shadows. Along with my Glilon assault rifle, I'm carrying an AN/PRC-77 field radio whose thirty-five-pound weight seems to be dragging me backward for every step I take. Each of the rest of the guys is covering the terrain on either side of the road with his Galil assault rifle. In addition to his rifle, each man has a "platoon weapon" as part of his equipment—a 52-millimeter mortar, an RPG-7 rocket-propelled grenade, or LAW antitank weapon.

3

Forty-two hours in motion or lying still, hunting or waiting for the enemy that Army Intelligence radioed was moving toward us. Now it's four forty-five in the morning and we are on our way back to our base, breathing cool dust instead of hot, putting one foot forward, then the other, tripping over ruts, aching, walking, breathing hard.

Funny about David, a huge, square-built American who, because of his size, was naturally issued one of the platoon machine guns in basic training. These are big, heavy weapons that are complicated to work, and a machine gunner has a very important place in any attack strategy. David's problem was that every time we went through a mock attack, he messed up the orders that needed to be relayed. First the sergeants, then the rest of us decided that he was stupid because he just couldn't seem to get them straight. Then Eli, our platoon commander, a quality leader, took David aside. "Listen," he said, "the point about a charge is to take the enemy. If the relay commands bother you in Hebrew, shout them in English, but keep moving." On the very next exercise, there was David, an Israel Defense Force soldier, racing up a hill shouting "Charge!" like an American cavalry officer, while his Israeli buddies, understanding his speed and his manner rather than his command, raced up the hill after him. From that moment on, he's been a brilliant machine gunner.

As the sun comes up, we move almost instinctively farther apart from each other, from night into day formation, as Ehud whispers, *"Revachim, revachim,* spread out, spread out."

We should be too tired to move, but by now, our muscles respond to our training and our surroundings more than to any feelings of our own. All of basic training is designed to make us do more than we can by changing our sense of what our own limits might be. Now our eyes feel propped open. I can hardly blink. We move in a fuzzy ambience, as if we were walking through radio static, our hearing and seeing slightly distorted.

All of last night we lay on the side of a hill waiting in ambush for the enemy that was reportedly on the way. We lay on our stomachs in a circle, linked leg to leg, doing what we could to maintain absolute silence. Overhead, the bright stars flickered. From the pace of their breathing, I could tell who was awake and who was asleep. Every so often I heard the rustling of paper as someone unwrapped a snack and the crunch as it was eaten. Ta'ami bars . . . chocolate coating over hard kernels that pretend to be puffed rice, fused together with the barest minimum of caramel syrup. Or Egozi bars, whipped nougat surrounding whole hazel nuts, the entire mixture covered with chocolate. Or maybe Bisli, thick curly chips that come in garlic, barbecue, or felafel flavors. What I'd have given for a Snickers bar.

We waited, clutching our weapons, forbidden to leave the perimeter of our ambush. Our nerves were stretched to the breaking point because this time we were not on a training exercise. The terrorists coming our way were armed, and if we met, they and we would shoot to kill.

I wondered who they might be. Tired as I was, I had no trouble imagining them in detail. Every time I pictured one of them, he always appeared older and bigger and scruffier than the guys around me. Unshaven, with a kefiyah around his neck and shoulders. A sweating, dusty, grim-eyed, looming figure with bandoliers across his chest, a knife between his teeth, a grenade in one hand and a Kalachnikov assault rifle in the other.

My mind drifted and I felt myself in danger of falling asleep. *Slurp.* It was the Frenchman, Josh, to my left, doing what he could to finish off the water in his water bottle.

"Water bottle," I said, the way one pinches oneself to stay awake. "Water bottle."

When you go on patrol, you fill your canteens to the top so

they won't gurgle. For the same reason, anyone who drinks from a canteen has to drink it all or have a friend finish it. This was a lesson that Josh learned through hard experience. Two nights in a row during basic training, he failed to fill his canteen to the top. At inspection, Lieutenant Eli put Josh's canteen to his ear and shook it. "What's this?" he said. "What's this I hear? Blurp-blurp, glug glug. No, soldier. That won't do. No blurp-blurp, glug-glug on patrol. What do you think these are," he said, shaking the canteen, "casta-nets? If they're castanets, dance me a samba. Now. Do it. Dance."

And there poor was Josh, a Frenchman, clumping away as he did his best to imitate a samba while the rest of us sup-pressed our laughter.

But that wasn't all. When the dancing was done Lieuten-ant Eli said, "Thank you, soldier. And tonight, your job is to fill the canteens for the entire platoon. And this time, no castanets. *Muvan,* understood?"

Josh understood. At the end of a seventeen-hour day, he was up until late into the night, lining up seventy-four can-teens, moving down the rows, filling each one to the top, then shaking it to make sure there was no gurgle.

From our hillside ambush we could see the lights of the various Arab villages that surrounded us. Some of them were Shiite, some of them Christian. Hezbollah and Amal ter-rorists hide in the Shiite villages while the Christians are on our side. Behind us and to the left, we could see the lights of a Jewish border kibbutz where my friend Nathan, who works in the orchard, lives.

The hours passed slowly, but there was no sign of any terrorists and it was clear that they had either missed us or were somewhere else. Then, at four o'clock, just before dawn, the radio handset strapped to my helmet crackled. "Watermelon One, Watermelon One, this is Romeo. Pepsi.

Pepsi." I reached for the other handset and passed it to the company commander. It was headquarters sending a Pepsi call, meaning "Return to base." Slowly, we pulled ourselves together, checking that no one had left any candy wrappers that might betray the fact that we had been there. Then we headed back to camp.

And that is why we are slogging along the rutted road to T., with the morning sun already warming our necks. With the advancing heat we feel the weight of our ballistic helmets and Kevlar flak jackets. It is as if we were carrying a portable sauna along with all the rest of our equipment. Soon we will be in camp. We can shed our gear. We can flop.

As we approach our base camp overlooking the village of T., we pass the UN post manned by blond Norwegians wearing pressed green uniforms, sunny giants, all of whom stand six feet ten inches tall and whose shined shoes sparkle in the sunlight. Despite the fact that only last week a stray .50 caliber shell from one of our firing exercises blew a hole in their water tank, they wave briskly, cheerfully at us. We in turn wave a bedraggled greeting as we pass.

With a hundred yards to go before we come to the barbed wire perimeter of our base, we break into a run. It is a company tradition to run the last hundred yards after completing a patrol. The idea is to beat the company commander back to the base, but he beats us every time. Of course he is carrying the lightest load, if you don't count the burden of command.

Then we are inside the gates, but instead of falling out we are hustled off for a two-hour road-clearing assignment. On our way back to the base, we get a radio message that a patrol from our ally, the South Lebanon Army (SLA), made contact with a group of five terrorists carrying five Kalachnikovs, two LAW antitank weapons, twenty-two pounds of TNT, and an RPG. In the ensuing fire fight, three of the terrorists were killed and two were captured and brought back to our base.

Inside our base I run into Tal, a tall dark soldier, the son of an Iraqi father and a South African mother. Tal, who is standing guard duty, points to an ambulance where the prisoners are. He moves close to me, but not too far away from the shelf on which his MAG machine gun rests and underneath which his transistor radio is pulsating with the jazz music he adores.

"You guys don't know how lucky you are," he says.

"Lucky? After forty-two hours on patrol?"

"Yeah," he says, "Listen. You almost had yourselves a little jam session. That's the bunch you went out to get. Somehow, in the dark, they got past you and set up an ambush on the road just eighty yards from your position. If it hadn't been for two things, you'd have had a bad night, mon."

"What the hell are you talking about?"

"Wait a minute," he says, moving back toward his transistor. In principle, no soldier is allowed to listen to music while he's on guard, but since that's a rule too hard to follow, and Walkmans are clearly dangerous, we have decided that a compromise is a small transistor. After all, if it's not stereo, it isn't really music. Tal is never out of listening distance from his.

"Yeah. Lucky. Twice. First, they were slow getting their heavy equipment set up. Then, just about the time they had you in their sights, this *chuku* squad of SLAs stumbled on them. The survivors are in there," he says, pointing to an ambulance.

There is a crowd of guys bunched around the open rear doors. I push my way through to the tailgate. I'm surprised by what I see. At first, in fact, I think I may have made some kind of mistake. What I see are two pale, skinny kids, both dressed only in clean white jockey shorts. One of them, his belly and one leg heavily bandaged, is lying unconscious on a stretcher on the left side of the ambulance, his face toward the wall. The other, who can't be more than seventeen years old, is sitting in a crouch on the other stretcher. One of his legs is bandaged. As I stare at him, he becomes aware of me and lifts his eyes to meet mine.

Stripped of his arsenal he is such a kid. He is unshaven all right—he looks as if he hasn't yet begun to shave. And his eyes are dark, but they are not angry slits; they are wide with fear. Is he afraid of me? Am I afraid of him?

As I look at him, I don't really feel anything against this guy. And I've been out in the night preparing to kill him. And he, who has no idea who I am, was out there getting ready to kill me.

2

We're doing our ninety-kilometer (fifty-five-mile) march over dirt paths and roads from Paratroopers Monument near Tel Nof to Ammunition Hill, a memorial site in Jerusalem that commemorates the 1967 battle for the city. Marching is a great way to understand how relative fatigue and distance can be. The first couple of marches we took, we built up to six miles and were exhausted after the first three. Later, when we did fifteen-mile marches, we were worn out after ten. When we did thirty, we were beat after twenty. And now, we've just done thirty miles almost without feeling it. Almost, because it suddenly hits me that we still have twenty-five miles to go, mostly uphill to Jerusalem. "Ascending to Jerusalem." The idea of a march is that no matter what's bothering you, you keep going. It's still hard, and we still have to keep going.

Fatiguing though it is, this march is different from all the others. For one thing, this is the longest march and the culmination of my paratroop training. This morning I made my last training jump, got my wings, packed my gear, and at

sundown, here I am, on my way toward the red beret that's
waiting for me at the end of this march. With it, I'll be a full-
fledged paratrooper. For another, there is no night discipline
keeping us muzzled, silent. In fact, loaded though we are
with full equipment, one of us is carrying a gigantic boom
box jacked up to full volume.

And on this march we can sing and talk. And what a relief
that is. OK, so I have an aching back, aching feet, but now I
get to groan, "Oh, my aching back. Oh, my aching feet."

It's now midnight. Again, I'm carrying the field radio
which, heavy though it is, isn't quite as heavy as the load the
rest of the guys are carrying. Each guy, in addition to carrying a gun and ammunition webbing holding eight full magazines, is part of a twelve-man team carrying a soldier on a
stretcher—some lucky guy hurt just enough in parachute
training that he can't make the march. Fortunately for my
buddies, the guy they're carrying, Manni, happens also to be
very light.

There's an irony about Manni. The guy on the stretcher is
called a *tayass,* a pilot, and Manni spent nine months training to be a pilot before he was dropped from the course.
Here, though, he is a good *tayass,* staying awake throughout
the march. Wearing his helmet, he lies strapped to the
stretcher and encourages the guys carrying him. Twelve men
are assigned to our stretcher but only four can carry it at one
time. So Manni, at one-minute intervals, calls *"Psst!"* as a
signal for the guys to switch.

At two or three o'clock in the morning we start up a long
ascent with two thirds of our march behind us. Twenty miles
to go. Far above us, on what would ordinarily be the horizon,
I see a golden halo which cannot possibly be formed by
anything but the lights of Jerusalem. Just then, the guy with
the boom box tunes in on a golden oldie station and I hear:

Those were the days, my friend
We thought they'd never end
We'd sing and dance
For ever and a day . . .

It's Mary Hopkins singing as I heard her singing it in 1968. But back then I heard it in Hebrew:

Hayu yamim chaver
Ach hem avru maher . . .

The summer of 1968, I am eight years old, a third grader, living in San Francisco. I have a five-and-a-half-year-old sister, and I haven't a clue that my life is about to change, though as I think back, I have the feeling that I must have heard the word "sabbatical" and something about book contracts being tossed about a lot that summer.

Then bang, I am yanked out of my comfortable routine, and my parents, my sister, and I are on a Pan Am flight to Tel Aviv. Well, what does an eight-year-old know? Whatever's happening to his family seems normal. If your family happens to get up and move to Israel, that's what families do. Anyhow, that's what mine did.

I remember the long taxi ride from the airport as a time of bright light and heat. The long climb past Latrun up the winding road that ascends to Jerusalem. The dark green of the forest on either side, glimpses of the burned-out makeshift armored trucks that the Israelis used in '47 as they sought to break the Arab blockade of Jerusalem. Those hulks, painted red, are still there, serving as a war memorial.

Then, we are in a cool, blue room with arched ceilings. The American Colony Hotel in the Arab section of Jerusalem. There are four high beds and we all lie down for a short nap from which, five or six hours later, we wake groggy with jet lag.

Slowly I develop a sense of Jerusalem. It's hotter than San Francisco. Drier, much less green. But everywhere there are sharp clear colors. The field stone with which Jerusalem houses are built give the city a golden aura. San Francisco is "the cool gray city of love," and here I am, in Jerusalem the gold.

Walking into class for the first time, I very soon learn that Israeli kids aren't like the ones back home. They are more inquisitive, rowdier. They surround me, asking questions in a language I don't yet understand. They're used to newcomers. There are immigrants from scores of countries in Israel, and these kids have either come from someplace else themselves, or have parents, uncles, aunts, or cousins who have.

Right away, the teacher teams me up with Yossi who, twenty years later, will still be my friend. Yossi assumes responsibility for me for the first few months, during which I study Hebrew in the morning and then do regular classroom work in the afternoon. I can't remember just when it was that I suddenly started to understand the language and be understood.

After that, I settle in and am an eight-year-old like any other, though it seems to me that Israeli kids have more freedom than San Francisco kids. I am out at all hours. We do a lot of exploring on weekends. This, despite the fact that the War of Attrition is on and there is a rash of artillery bombardments on the border and terrorist bomb attacks following Israel's victories in the Six Day War. I become aware of all this in only the most indirect ways. In San Francisco, our teachers used to put us through earthquake drills where we were taught to hide under our desks; here we have air raid drills during which we all file down into the school's bomb shelter. And our teachers warn us about something called "button bombs" that El Fatah is said to be sprinkling on school playgrounds. Once, a bomb is found in a felafel stand across the street from my school, and I stand in the

crowd that gathers to watch the bomb squad defuse it. And
of course there is a guard at the front gate of my school who
checks people's bags to see that they aren't carrying explo-
sives. But as an eight-year-old, I simply assume that that's
how things are everywhere. I have no distinct sense that we
are living under siege, or that life in Jerusalem is any different from anyplace else.

No. That can't be true. There is the Old City. In Rehavia,
the district in Jerusalem where my family lives, the ambience is Westernized middle class. But in the Old City, the
streets are narrow and winding. People speak Arabic and
there are men in kefiyas, women in long tribal dresses, Fran-
ciscan monks in brown cassocks, and Greek orthodox priests
with their black robes and cylindrical hats. And, especially
on Saturdays, Hassidic Jews wearing fur hats and kaftans as
they hurry to or from prayer at the Western Wall.

And always, there are the merchants standing beside their
shops calling, "Allo, allo. You don't have to buy. Just take a
look." There are the smells of food cooking on kerosine
stoves in dark little shops; colorful spices displayed in open
boxes: orange-yellow saffron, green coriander, golden cumin,
green za'atar; whole vats of olives; brass pots of *sahleb,* clot-
ted milk; sticky piles of sesame seed and almond cakes;
gleaming golden-fried honey cakes. Everything in great
heaps: beans, cauliflowers, tomatoes, parsley, carrots, figs,
bananas.

I have my favorite merchant whom I visit every Saturday
morning. He is an old man on David Street who wears a fez
and who sits on a tiny stool beside a glass case from which
he sells antique coins. He speaks neither Hebrew nor English, and of course I speak no Arabic. But he is always
extremely patient with me and seems to take special pleasure
in laying out his brightest coins for me, though a kid with an
eight-year-old's allowance can hardly bring much profit.

From time to time I do get the feeling that life is a bit

graver than it is in San Francisco and that Arabs are somehow connected to that gravity. Whenever the beep beep that
signals the hourly newscast on the radio sounds, somebody
turns up the volume and everybody stops to listen. And because the country is so small, whenever there is a report of
someone being killed, there is always someone you know
who knows, or is related to, the victim or his family. And
that year, a lot of people are killed.

Finally there is the presence of the Israeli soldier. That
always seems serious to me. Very early, like the rest of the
kids in my *chevra*, my group, I learn to think of the Israeli
soldier as a hero. Sometimes a soldier comes to my school to
talk about his work or about the political situation. And
wherever I go, I see soldiers, their Uzis slung over their
shoulders. Like my classmates, I learn to distinguish between the yellow shoulder tags with brown cedar trees of the
Golani infantrymen, and the winged serpents of the para-
troops. We talk about soldiers a lot. This guy's uncle is a
paratrooper, that guy's brother is in the tank corps. Somebody else's father is a pilot—and that's even more important
than being the kid in my class who is the president's
nephew.

But for all of that, kids my age don't brood much about
the world of grown-ups. The big event of 1968 is the great
snowfall and we are all out in the streets and on the hillsides
throwing snowballs and improvising sleds.

> *Those were the days, my friend*
> *We thought they'd never end . . .*

Ammunition webbing, field radio, gun. The straps are bit-
ing into my flesh. Ascending to Jerusalem, twelve miles to
go.

For any Jew, the return to Israel is regarded as a spiritual
ascent; the same is true of the return to Jerusalem, which is

both a physical and a spiritual ascent. Leaving, or *yerida*, is regarded as descending. But these distinctions were not on my mind in the fall of 1969 when, to the surprise of my friends, my family "went down" to San Francisco.

> *We'd fight and never lose*
> *For we were young and sure to have our way.*

In 1973 we almost did lose, and we surely didn't have our way.

In 1973, my father gets another year-long leave of absence from San Francisco State University. I overhear long discussions between my parents about where we should go. My mother proposes Rio de Janeiro and my father is willing as long as we can drive down. For the next several months, the whole family is caught up in preparations for the trip. We trade in our Volkswagen hatchback for a Toyota Land Cruiser with four-wheel drive; we rummage army surplus stores for mosquito netting and machetes; we send off to AAA for road maps.

My grandmother, who every few years watches stoically as another of her children—especially my mother—goes wandering off around the world, stores our boxes in her basement.

Then problems crop up. My parents aren't thrilled about the prospect of enrolling me and my sister in a Catholic school, but learning Portuguese would cut too deeply into our schoolwork, and the Catholic school is the only English-speaking school nearby. Then my father gets another book contract, this time to write about Shabbetai Zvi, a seventeenth-century Jew who claimed he was the Messiah. The bulk of his research would take place in Israel and Turkey. But what finally convinces us is the triptyque we receive from AAA. There are enormous gaps along the solid black line representing the Pan-American Highway. The footnote reads "Due to be completed by 1980."

So, on the first of October, having sold the Land Cruiser and the mosquito netting, my father, my sister, and I arrive at the airport in Tel Aviv. My mother is scheduled to follow a month later, just as soon as she has finished her graduate degree at the University of California.

We arrive at night. This time, the ride to Jerusalem past the armored hulks and the forest has a more somber, even dreamlike, quality.

Again we settle into an apartment in Rehavia. This time, going to school is hardly disorienting at all. I walk into class and there is Yossi, on his feet, greeting me. And of course this time, there is no language problem. I feel fine.

We all feel fine. It is a lovely fall. The weather is bright and clear. We have arrived in Jerusalem during the days between Rosh Hashanah, the New Year, and Yom Kippur, the Day of Atonement. It is a time of year when Jews feel a great sense of renewal. For me, the time is especially auspicious. On the fifteenth of October I will be thirteen years old, the year in which, among Jews, a boy becomes a man.

On Saturday, October 6, Yom Kippur, we get back from synagogue about one o'clock in the afternoon. I have that peculiar empty feeling you get when you are fasting. I'm not so much hungry as passive. Waiting in slow motion for the sun to go down.

Then, at two o'clock, in the cool, shuttered apartment where we are lying down, I hear the high-pitched wail of an air raid siren.

The moments that follow seem fragmented. At first, my sister and I, remembering all of our school training, hide under the dining room table. Then, my sister peeks out the window and cries, "Hey, everybody's going to the bomb shelter." I look. She is right. Other people in our apartment building, old hands at bomb shelters, are on their way carrying transistor radios, candles, and little sacks of candy.

My father, my sister, and I follow the crowd. Every building in Israel has a bomb shelter and ours is small, musty, dusty, and dark. A single bare bulb sheds a vague light over the little crowd of us sitting on the wooden benches. One of our neighbors, a gentle middle-aged woman, sits opposite me holding a sealed bag of candy in her lap. I stare at the candy, hoping she will catch the look of longing in my eyes, but then I remember, it is Yom Kippur and I suppress my hunger. Meanwhile, the adults are busy listening to the radio, which is announcing, at fifteen-minute intervals, the news of the Syrian and Egyptian attack on Israel. In between newscasts come the call-up code names of Israeli Army units. These are the signals every reservist in Israel—all men between the ages of twenty-one and fifty-five—is listening for to tell him where he must report. Half an hour after we enter the bomb shelter, we hear the rising and falling wail of the all-clear and we go back to our apartment.

That night, my father, my sister, and I sit on the big bed in his bedroom. I'm about to be thirteen years old, and my sister is eleven. We know that something scary is happening because my father is asking us to help him make an adult decision.

"Look," he says. "I'm going to call your mother. She has to know what's going on. But I have to know how you feel about being here. What do you think? Do you want to go home?"

We sit on the bed, and for a moment there is no reply, but it is not because we are hesitating about our answer. It is just that we didn't know there was an option.

Finally, my sister says, "Tell Mom we want to stay."

"Yes," I say. "Tell her we want to stay."

Making an international phone call from Israel is never easy. Reaching my mother on the first day of the Yom Kippur War takes several hours of patient dialing. Finally, we have her on the line. Of course she has already heard the news of the war. "Are you all right?" she shouts, and Dad shouts back, "We're fine." Before he can tell her that we want to stay, she shouts, "I'll be right there. Be careful. Take care of yourselves. I'll be right there."

"Right there" takes some time. With the exception of El Al, every commercial airline that usually flies to Israel cancels its flights. El Al's flights are booked solid with reserve soldiers coming back to join their units. So my mother gets to us by a circuitous route: she flies to London and there gets preferential treatment on a flight to Tel Aviv by pleading with the agent that she wants to be in Jerusalem for her son's thirteenth birthday. Well, how can a Jewish airline stand between a mother and her son's bar mitzvah? She arrives on the fourteenth, the night before my birthday.

In this war, there is no Israeli euphoria. Both the Syrian attack on the Golan Heights and the Egyptian attack across the Suez Canal come perilously close to success. By the time the two attacks are contained and then rolled back, a great many young people, Jews and Arabs, have died. A week after the war begins, life in Israel feels chaotic. Some of my schoolmates don't come to school because a member of their family has been killed. Food hoarders rush the grocery stores, emptying out the shelves, though the government radio assures us that there is no shortage.

There are no young men in the streets, an eerie feeling. High school students are pressed into service to deliver the mail. They do their best. Sometimes the mail is delivered, sometimes it's days late. At school, we do very little studying. Instead, we spend our time filling up sandbags and taping windows to keep them from shattering. We learn to tell the difference between a sonic boom and an explosion. The explosion is crisper, more engulfing, and seems to hit you in the stomach. The sonic boom comes in clustered twin thuds. It is a boom-boom that hits you mostly in the ears.

Everything around us, in the first weeks of war, contributes to our sense of danger. It is not some allegorical danger. It's the boys and girls around me. Rehavia, my school. The Jerusalem in which we live. This block. This street.

And with the danger comes a longing for action. We thirteen-year-olds would give anything to be at the front helping out. We all want to be paratroopers. We all want to be pilots. We listen avidly to the stories of the exploits of our soldiers. Such and such a unit blows up a radar installation. Such and such a force succeeds in trapping the entire Egyptian Third Army. These men become our heroes. Our Judah Maccabees. Our Bar Kochbas.

The Yom Kippur War lasts eighteen days. Israel has again survived, but it has paid a heavy price. Two thousand five hundred and twenty-one young Israelis dead, and I can see for myself the sudden appearance in the streets of amputees and soldiers with bandaged arms or heads. The following spring, at Ma'aleh Hachamisha, the swimming pool my family goes to, I see the young amputees swimming in their awkward fashion.

It takes a while, but eventually civilian life resumes its normal course. The reservists are discharged from their units. Mailmen deliver the mail. We take the tape off the windows at school. People scrape the blackout paint off their automobile headlights. The songs on the radio are grimly optimistic. Yoram Gaon sings:

> *I promise you my little one*
> *That this will be the last war.*

Meanwhile Yossi, my best friend, and I lead our kids' lives. We string tin can telephones between our apartments.

We play Israeli Monopoly. He wins Trumpeldor Street; I win
Hertzl Avenue. My *kvutsah*, my crowd, goes off on a bike trip
to some caves near Bethlehem. On the way back we get lost
somewhere on the West Bank and are finally saved by a
bunch of Israeli soldiers in a jeep who, alerted by our anxious parents, have been out looking for us. I have resumed
my hopeless infatuation with Irit, whom I loved for the first
time when I was eight. In 1968 I would ask for extra candies
for my lunchbox so I could give them to her. She always
took the candy but spurned my love. She liked Raffi, a
skinny kid with blond hair and blue eyes whose bones jutted
out all over the place, and whose chin was too wide for his
face. He never thought to bring her candy. And now, at
thirteen, she is a classic Moroccan beauty: olive skin, almond eyes, long black hair. But she continues to spurn my
love. High school boys interest her—lanky guys in blue
shirts who think they look cool in their school uniforms.

On the fifteenth of May, 1974, three heavily armed terrorists
cross the Lebanese border and slip into Ma'alot, an Israeli
settlement where, in the settlement schoolhouse, they take
ninety children hostage. Some of the children escape by
jumping out of second-story windows. When troops from the
Golani brigade storm the school, the terrorists open fire,
killing twenty-five children before they themselves are
killed. On the TV news that night, I see pictures of the
soldiers carrying wounded children. I see the bullet-sprayed,
blood-stained walls of the school. Pictures of bereaved parents and still terrified children.

By the end of the year, there have been twelve such terrorist incursions into Israel.

In June, when I learn that my family is going back to San
Francisco, I ask to be allowed to stay in Israel.

"Why in the world would you want to do that?"

"So I can be a soldier when I grow up."

Nobody listens to thirteen-year-olds. When fall comes, there I am, back in San Francisco taking my first puffs on cigarettes with my American friends. Sometimes, we play at petty crime—breaking into empty homes on a dare and, a real coup, sneaking into a bank lobby at night.

It doesn't take long and I'm back to being an American in junior high, then in high school. I watch the miniseries "Roots" on TV, then "Holocaust." I study algebra, trigonometry. I read *The Bounty Trilogy, Exodus,* Jim Bouton's *Ball Four, Spider-Man* comics, and anything I can get my hands on by Jack London: *The Call of the Wild, The Sea Wolf.*

I'm an American kid and yet—a Jewish American. My father was raised Orthodox in an immigrant home in the Midwest. My mother grew up Reform in a modern academic family in California's central valley. The cultural compromise my parents arrived at was Conservative Judaism. Although not rigidly religious, they always try to instill Jewish tradition and values in our life. We celebrate the major holidays—belting out *Ma'oz Tsur,* "Rock of Ages," in front of the lighted menorah during Hannukah, and packing bologna sandwiches on matzo in our lunch bags at Passover. And on Friday night, after candle lighting and the Sabbath meal, I go with my family to services at Congregation Beth Shalom.

Rabbi White, more than anyone I have ever met, is imbued with the fire of a living Judaism. He is not driven by some rulebook-oriented creed. His Judaism, derived as it is from the great old books, manages not to have the smell of antiquity about it. It always seems new and urgent and capable of being described, as Rabbi Hillel said, while standing on one leg. The essence of it is this: "You shall be holy, for I, the Lord your God, am holy."

In June 1976, I return to Israel, this time on a synagogue-sponsored youth trip.

We get to Tel Aviv in the middle of June. Once again, I am in love, this time with a girl in our group of Egyptian descent. Her name is Michele. She, too, is a dark-haired beauty with olive skin and almond eyes.

The crowd I am with behaves like typical Americans, buying T-shirts that say Coca-Cola in Hebrew, taking pictures of everything in sight: Israelis on motorcycles, Israeli telephone poles, Israeli policemen. Because Israel has no minimum drinking age, I have my first legal drink—whiskey on the rocks, because that is all I know how to order. It tastes terrible.

We visit the various borders of Israel. We go disco dancing on the beaches in Eilat; we fill bottles with multicolored sand that we find in the Negev; we *mizdangeff*, that is, we promenade along Diezengoff Street in Tel Aviv, checking out the cafés and shops.

We have an Israeli counselor named Aryeh. When we climb Mount Sinai, he dresses up as Moses and sets off an army smoke grenade to create very impressive visual effects. With him, we visit the Adam Bridge on the Israeli-Jordanian border and wave at Jordanian troops. Then we climb the Golan Heights.

There, I start to dig around in an old bunker and find an army boot. I think it's kind of funny that somebody would leave a single boot in a bunker. I pull it out and hear something rattling inside. When I turn the boot upside down, a handful of bones falls out. I look up and see that Aryeh has a pained look on his face. Later, I learn why: his brother was killed on these heights in 1973.

Telling us about how his brother died in a tank battle seems to open him up. He describes his own combat experience: defensive fighting in trenches in the Sinai; house-to-house-fighting in the city of Suez; attacks on bunkers like the one we have just seen.

Then he smiles. "Let me tell you about my big war wound." We all lean forward. "John Wayne gave it to me."

"John Wayne?"

"Listen," he says. "You know, taking these bunkers was always bloody work. When you attack a bunker, the first thing you do is toss in a grenade, then you go in, spraying machine-gun fire. Sometime in 1973, before my army duty, I had seen a war movie in which John Wayne pulls the firing pin from his grenade with his teeth. Well, I got through the war unscathed, except for one thing. Movie firing pins come out a hell of a lot more easily than real ones and I chipped this damned tooth imitating the Duke."

On July 4, 1976, my group is in Caesaria. It is America's Bicentennial, and we are on the beach celebrating. In the broiling Mediterranean sun, we whoop and holler and shoot off firecrackers. In the presence of Roman ruins, we praise General Washington, the Minute Men, and the Continental Army, and we drink watery Israeli beer.

That night, we get the news that the rescued Entebbe hostages have arrived in Israel.

The Entebbe story began on June 27 when a French A-300B Airbus, Flight 139 departing from Athens and carrying 256 passengers, was hijacked eight minutes after take-off. The team of hijackers, who got past lax Athens security measures, included two Arabs and two Germans, a man and a woman who were members of the Bader-Meinhof gang. The hijackers called themselves the "Ché Guevara Cell of the Haifa Unit" of the PFLP (Popular Front for the Liberation of Palestine). They forced the French crew to fly the plane to Benghazi, in Libya, where it was refueled, and then to Entebbe, Uganda, where ten more Arab terrorists joined the hijackers.

Then the hijackers sorted out their hostages. Those with "Jewish names" were kept as prisoners. The non-Jews were released the next day and flown to Paris. That left 103 Jewish—not Israeli, Jewish—hostages. The French crew, to its credit, elected to stay with them.

And then came the rescue at Entebbe. The Israeli government—which did not need to respond, since the plane was French and in Ugandan territory—mounted an operation to rescue the endangered Jews. That operation has gone down in history as a model of imaginative and heroic military action. Fifty-seven minutes from the time the commandos made their first contact with Ugandan troops guarding the terminal building, the terrorists were dead and the hostages were freed and out of Entebbe. It was a brilliant raid, but it had its price. Lt. Colonel Yoni Natanyahu, the leader of the raid, was killed, as was Dora Bloch, an Englishwoman.

For me, Entebbe illuminated, in the most practical way, the meaning of the Jewish history that I got in bits and pieces from Rabbi White's Friday night sermons and from my two-year-long stays in Israel: Two thousand years of Jewish homelessness, the disaster of the Holocaust, and the establishment of the State of Israel formed a design. There *was* a Jewish people, and it was no longer adrift in history, no longer powerless. There was a Jewish state, and when Jews were endangered anywhere in the world, that state acted.

It is July 4, American Independence Day, but it is also July 4, the day the rescued hostages arrive in Israel. The next day, our tour bus picks up half a dozen hitchhiking soldiers. They have evidently been on some exhausting duty. Their clothes are dusty, stained. And the minute they sit down, they lean their heads against the windows of the bus and fall asleep.

I am sixteen years old, and I know that one day I will be one of them.

And here I am in 1987, as tired and bedraggled as they were. Marching to get my red beret in Jerusalem.

The first ten hours of this march were OK: in the cool night and on comparatively flat ground, they flew by. The next four hours were painful, but I could manage them. We marched first through the false dawn, then the real one. Now the temperature starts to rise and we are marching on concrete and asphalt. Our pace slows to a crawl. Each time I put a foot down, I feel like I'm walking on coals. I have needles in my toes, needles in my heels. I'm so wet with sweat that I seem to be swimming inside my clothes. I've lost sensation in the palms of my hands, and my shoulder straps feel like hacksaws sawing their way through my shoulder blades.

We reach the outskirts of Jerusalem when the boom box, from whose innards Madonna has been blaring "Material Girl," suddenly gives out. There is a last burst of static and the batteries go dead.

I look over at Tommy, surprised to see that he is still going strong. I had worried about him when we started. He's a tall string bean of a guy from Manchester, England, who insists on calling himself a Mancunian, and whose size fourteen feet have a habit of walking off without him. His usual way of dealing with a march is to curse it from the time we take off to the time we finish. But he always makes it. This time, too, he is cursing as he carries the MAG. He's cursing his feet, the army, the passersby, but he keeps walking. And as Tommy curses the march, David his buddy, marching beside him, curses Tommy. It is their usual arrangement.

As we pass through Rehavia, a woman on the sidewalk, seeing Manni being carried on his stretcher, comes running up.

"I'm a nurse," she cries. "I'm a nurse. Can I help?"

David, sweating as a stretcher bearer, interrupts his cursing to say, "Thanks, lady. I just wish you could. We're going to Ammunition Hill." She gets the message, smiles, and wishes us luck.

We are on our last mile and now young women, girlfriends

of some of the guys in the unit, join the march and our spirits instantly rise. With only a hundred yards to go, we discover a last reserve of strength and run right to the top of the hill. We've made it.

We do stretching exercises so we won't cramp up. Parents and friends and kibbutz comrades surround us. Our company commander, Lieutenant Shuki, who has done this march only four times, comes up and puts the company in U-formation by platoon.

"Congratulations," he says. "We made it. You'll be happy to know that the company behind us isn't due for a couple of hours yet. You've made it in sixteen hours. [We would learn later that it took C-company twenty-two hours.] You certainly deserve the right to wear the red beret."

With that, he calls out the names of the four people in the company who have done particularly well on the march, and personally sets their red berets on their heads. One of the men honored this way is Mario, an Italian Jew who, in basic training, was considered a *fuckyonaire* by the officers—and now here he is, finally being recognized as the good soldier we knew he was.

Lieutenant Shuki then turns each platoon over to its platoon commander. Ari, our commander, goes down the line and sets a red beret on each of our heads. *"Mazal tov,"* he says. *"Magia lecha.* You deserve it."

"Toda," I reply. "Thanks."

At the celebratory picnic that follows, I sit under a tree, turning the beret round and round with my fingers. This is something I've wanted for a long time. Well, now that I've got it, was it worth it? I've got blisters, sore shoulders, bad legs, and a chafing crotch. In the last week I've seen guys faint, cry, break legs and backs, and curse the day they were born. But yeah, I think it's worth it.

Hell, after a year and three months, I've got a red beret and wings.

3

October 1, 1987

Dear Ariella,

Well, it's over. Ninety kilometers in sixteen hours. This after a week of parachute jumps.

It's 7:30 on Yom Kippur morning. It's so strange to be here—so dreamlike. Everyone is walking like they're on the moon. The pains in our muscles and feet should be sufficient penitence for the sins of the past year. Even so, about half of us are fasting. The others are plowing through the *chuparim* [goodies] they got from their families after the march on Thursday.

Meanwhile, I miss you terribly, but I feel better because I know I'll see you on Wednesday. There'll be the candle burning softly. And you. Then Judy Collins singing us gently to sleep.

See you then. All my love.

A.

Today is the day after Yom Kippur. Yesterday, the Book of Life was sealed for the year. Now we go back to work and attend to the responsibilities that accompany our newly acquired red beret and parachute wings. Anyone who has finished the parachute course wears his wings against a blue background. A course instructor wears his wings on a white background; commandos trained to jump into water get to wear theirs over a black background. Wings worn over red are rare; only those who have jumped in combat are entitled to that distinction and no one has jumped in combat since the Battle of the Mitla Pass in the Sinai campaign of 1956. Because I earned my wings in the paratrooper brigade, I am entitled to wear them over a green background. So I have to modify the insignia.

Ever since the picnic at which we celebrated the completion of our ninety-kilometer march, the guys have been asking their relatives to bring them empty plastic Sprite bottles. What we do is peel away the blue plastic backing of our wings and lay it as a pattern over a piece of green plastic from the Sprite bottle. Then using an Exacto knife, we carefully, carefully cut a replica of the blue backing, and *voilà,* we have the appropriate backing for our wings.

That's not all. The code of the combat soldier is that he has to look rugged, and our red berets look too new. To rectify this breach of military etiquette, we have to make them look as combat-worn as we are. This is a long process. First we cut out their satin linings, then we soak the berets in water, after which we put them, folded down the middle, under our mattresses and sleep on them overnight. In the morning, the creased berets look as if we have been carrying them in our pockets for months. But they're still too shiny, so we soak them again and lay them out in the sun to dry for the rest of the day, turning them over from time to time to make sure they dry evenly. As the water evaporates, so does some of the color. By the end of the day, our red berets have an appropriately rugged earthy tone. We now look as if we had worn them as each of us, singlehandedly, reunified Jerusalem, knocked the Syrians off the Golan Heights, and rescued the hostages at Entebbe.

Before we get to strut, however, we're off on patrol—to Jenin, a large Arab town in the northern part of the West Bank. The bazaar and market areas are in the center of town; we are quartered in the Military Administration compound right next to it. There is a UN-run refugee camp within walking distance. We patrol through the bazaar then out to the camp and back. Our orders are to stay out of the camp unless there is trouble.

We soon have trouble. Later, the headline will read STONES, PETROL BOMBS AND IRON BARS HURLED AT TROOPS. What actually happens is this: It's a hot day, the sun is glaring off the white limestone buildings, and some damn machine in the town quarry is pounding away. We pass donkeys carrying firewood, sacks of grain, or jerry cans filled with kerosine. Housewives are out, carrying their plastic shopping baskets filled with groceries, vegetables, and fruit.

There are six of us on patrol with Ari, our platoon commander. We walk in staggered formation on either side of the road, keeping plenty of distance between us, because a couple of months earlier in Bethlehem an Arab tried to run an Israeli patrol down with his car. Two of the guys were hurt and more of them would have been if they hadn't been keeping their distances.

Then we get a radio call to get over to the refugee camp. A rock has been hurled at one of our jeep patrols. We are off and running.

Each of us has an assault rifle, eight magazines in his *ephod* (ammunition webbing), two tear gas grenades, three rubber-bullet grenades, a helmet, and a billy club. We are combat ready, prepared to confront any enemy. Six fighters

armed, tensed and ready for action, with permission to enter
the camp and break up a riot.

Well, we sweep in all right, with fingers on triggers, and
around the very first corner, boom! We engage the enemy.

Their average age is six. A couple of the leaders may be
eight. One guy, undoubtedly a paid PLO agent from Beirut,
is ten. They look at us threateningly. We look at them. What
is needed is appropriate action. Now. At once. And so I
make a horrible face, stick out my tongue, and yell, "Boo!"

Sure enough, they scatter and run for home.

I finally get to strut. On my weekend leave, rather than
rushing home to Kfar Hamaccabi, the kibbutz near Haifa
that has adopted me, I decide to spend the afternoon in
Jerusalem. Still stiff from the long march, I walk carefully to
avoid putting my muscles out of shape. But I walk with an
inner glow. This is the first time that I am wearing my dress
uniform with my paratrooper's wings and red beret. I am on
my way to the Old City, to the Western Wall.

Standing before those stones, assault rifle slung over my
shoulder, I start to pray the *Shehechiyanu*, a prayer of
thanks, but my mind is wandering. Proud as I am, I feel a
little ambivalent. I remember the image I had of the paratrooper before I joined the Army. It was the one in the
famous photo that David Rubinger took in 1967 of the paratroopers who had unified Jerusalem looking up in awe at the
Wall. They were clean and alert, their fight was just, and
they had performed brilliantly against overwhelming odds.
They were soldiers whose motives and whose arms were
pure.

Now, after a year and three months in the army, I am one
of them. But as I step through the picture, I find that the
issues are more clouded. The Rubinger picture has only two
dimensions. I found, as no doubt those soldiers did before
me, that there is a third dimension—and it's made up of

ambiguity and pain. I've discovered that facing a three-di-
mensional reality is no easy task. But at least I'm there. At
least I know.

My reverie is broken by a tourist who taps me on the
shoulder. "Soldier, do you mind if I take your picture?"

On the way out of the Old City I call Khalid, my Palestinian friend in Nablus, and ask him to meet me in Jerusalem.
Two hours later we are having lunch in a café on Ben
Yehudah Street. I am full of myself. I tell him about the
jumps, the long march; I show him my wings and he can't
help seeing the beret. I remember a comment his sister once
made when I was at their house in civilian clothes. "What
color beret do you wear?" she asked.

"A black beret and red boots," I replied, and she burst
out laughing. "What's so funny?" I asked.

"A black beret, red boots, a green uniform, and white
skin. You're a walking Palestinian flag."

I notice as we talk that Khalid seems a little restrained,
muted. He does what he can to be glad for me but I can tell
that something is bothering him. Finally I say, "What's up?
What's wrong?"

"I just got out of jail after eighteen days detention."

I feel as if I have been punched. All this while, he's been
listening to me, not as a Palestinian activist, just as my
friend, doing his best not to spoil my pleasure in my achievements. Now, suddenly, I have to do for him what he has
done for me—listen to his grief, his description of beatings
and physical humiliation. Not as an Israeli soldier having to
defend the policies that led to his arrest. Just as his friend.

"Why? What were the charges?"

"I don't know . . ."

I first met Khalid in the Fall of 1982. I was a "Zionist on
fire" at San Francisco State University, and he was a Pales-

tinian activist at U.C. Berkeley, right across the bay. But the story starts earlier.

In 1978, I graduated from high school and went off to New York University. I felt unmotivated, floundering. I barely lasted out the year. Finally, I figured I should take some time off and do something else, so I joined the U.S. Merchant Marine, shipping out of San Francisco as a deckhand.

On my first day at sea, I sat on the afterdeck with my shipmates eating Del Monte pineapple that had spilled from a shipment on the previous voyage. With every swallow of pineapple, I tried to suppress the seasickness that comes to most new sailors.

The guys around me were all older—the youngest in his forties, the rest in their fifties. They all drank heavily, and some rambled on about their hatred of women, blacks, foreigners, officers. Two or three were certifiably crazy. One of them complained that swarms of butterflies were attacking him, though the nearest butterfly was two hundred nautical miles to the east; another shouted threats all day at invisible enemies.

Because I was an "ordinary seaman," I was teamed up with the "able-bodied seaman" on my watch, who showed me the ropes. He was a fifty-eight-year-old black man named Howell from Mobile, Alabama. He taught me how to tie knots, how to chip paint and then repaint, how and where to hide from our bo'sun, and how to stand watch, the best part of the day for me.

For four hours my job was just to keep my eyes open for ships or whales or any other obstruction that might endanger our ship. I had the four to eight watch, the star watch, so that I was on in the morning and at night. At night in the lower latitudes, since I was the only man on deck, I stood my watch stark naked under the stars and sang with all my might to the dolphins playing in the ship's wake on either side of the bow.

I carried this practice of singing over onto my second ship, where, though I was not aware of it, there was a two-way intercom hooked up between me and the bridge. On the third night of the voyage, the intercom crackled and I heard the voice of the second mate: "Wolf, we're going to do a lot more watches together. If we're both going to make it, you're going to have to learn to shut the fuck up." The dolphins were out of luck.

I enjoyed my year at sea. I visited Japan, Korea, Guam, and Hawaii. I saw the hectic ports of Yokohama and the red-light districts of Pusan. But mostly what delighted me was the sea itself. One of my landlocked friends wanted to know what was so great about sailing. "All you've got is the sea and the sky." And he was right, but I never knew before how many shades of blue sky there were in the course of a single day. And at night, how many shades of black.

The moods of the sea are expressed in color and motion. Calm, the sea is every tint of blue; in storms it has an equal number of grays and greens and blacks. Swells toss the ship; waves sweep over it. A huge metal structure when it's tied to the dock, the ship turns feather light and insignificant when it is in the grip of a storm.

Being Jewish at sea wasn't much of a problem for me. The only overt anti-Semite was Sparks, the radio operator, who complained of an international conspiracy of Jewish radio men who wouldn't let him broadcast on certain bands. But holidays demanded some ingenuity on my part. Before we left Seattle, I had spent several hours in a taxi hopping from one supermarket to another trying to find matzos so I would be prepared when Passover overtook the ship in mid-Pacific.

So I had three pounds of matzos. The question was how to make a seder. When I asked Jimmy Cohen in the engine room to join me, he laughed and said, "I haven't done anything religious in forty years. I'm not about to start now. Sorry." That left me, alone, to celebrate the exodus from Egypt. I asked the captain to lend me his Bible. "I hope you find what you're looking for," he said, as he handed me his King James Version, utterly indifferent to why I wanted it.

So I sat in my cabin, two decks down, and asked myself, "Why is this night different from all other nights?" Afterward, in reply, I read the Book of Exodus, and washed down my matzo with four shots of Howell's Jack Daniel's whiskey.

My last ship let me off in New Orleans. I found a job as a midnight bellman in a five-star hotel on Bourbon Street and took a couple of courses at the University of New Orleans.

New Orleans is a party town and Bourbon Street is the party's center. The party runs on alcohol and money. And there's always good music. Rock, country, blues, Cajun, and fifty kinds of jazz—from Dixieland to fusion.

Working the graveyard shift at the hotel, I met drug dealers, prostitutes, scam artists, middle-American business people looking for the party, and oil-rich 3 A.M.'ers from Texas who, when the bars in Houston closed at 2 A.M. on Friday and Saturday, hopped into their private jets, and flew to New Orleans so that, by 3 A.M., they could be in the French Quarter, where the bars stay open all night.

It was an interesting but not very satisfying year. I wanted to travel again. I also began to suspect that I wanted to go to school full time.

In April, just as the weather was getting muggy, I went to see a performance of the Hassidic Song Festival at the Jewish Community Center. The performers were a group of young Israelis who did a show of modern song and dance based on Hassidic or biblical themes. Their Israeli vibrancy reminded me of how good I feel when I'm around people speaking Hebrew.

I went into the lobby and found a display of pamphlets

describing programs for American college students in Israel. The one that looked best was called Kibbutz–University Semester—a summer language course combined with work on a kibbutz named Kfar Hamaccabbi, and a semester at Haifa University. In July 1981, I returned to Israel.

Kfar Hamaccabbi was founded in 1937 by Eastern European immigrants. The kibbutz has citrus orchards, cotton and corn fields, fish ponds, dairy cows, and a small tire retread factory. As many as three hundred of us might eat together in the dining room. All the things that city people do for themselves—laundry, shopping, bookkeeping, paying taxes, and child care—are done on a kibbutz-wide scale. Each kibbutz member has a vote, and members elect committees to administer the day-to-day business. Though no one is paid a salary, everyone has access to something called "the budget," for money with which to defray ongoing small expenses. The amount of this allowance varies according to the size of one's family.

When I work in the cotton fields or in the grapefruit groves, I rise at four every morning, six days a week, and am finished with my work at two. I particularly enjoy my morning ritual among the grapefruit with my friends Steve and Nancy, two other American volunteers. At five or five-thirty, when the first sunbeams penetrate the cool groves, we stop work and, forming a sophisticated barber shop trio, look up and sing the Beatles song:

> *Here comes the sun,*
> *Little darling,*
> *Here comes the sun*
> *I say "It's all right."*

That done, we go back to work.

We are eight volunteers from all over the States and at

various stages of college study. Each of us is adopted by a
kibbutz family, which becomes our link to the rest of the
kibbutz. Our families invite us for coffee in the afternoons.
We sit with our families in the dining room for the Friday
evening (Shabbat) meal, and can be asked to participate in
other family occasions—birthdays, bar mitzvahs, weddings.

I am adopted by the Konnello family, who have been
kibbutz members for fifteen years. Yehuda, the father, is an
Egyptian, while Nehama, his wife, comes from a Polish family. They met while still in high school. They fell in love and
were married long before Eastern-Western unions became
common. Having dinner at their house is a special treat—
both of them are master cooks and display the best Egyptian
and Polish cuisine at their table. Where else in the kibbutz
could I have kubeh and gefilte fish at the same meal?

The Konnellos have two children, a daughter, Idit, who is
married and lives in Netanya, and a son, Ron, who is three
years my junior. Like his father, Ron is a short, muscular
guy; unlike him, Ron wears his brown hair long, kibbutz
style. Ron and I, designated at the beginning as adoptive
brothers, become in fact very close friends. We date together, hang out together. The two of us work in the cotton
fields. He teaches me to drive a tractor and works with me
laying long thin aluminum irrigation pipes that get infernally
hot in the summer sun. Since young kibbutz members generally volunteer for combat units, he sometimes shares with
me his anxieties about his coming army service. He isn't
sure he can hack it, and he is afraid he may be injured or
killed.

In the fall of 1981, Steve and I share a dormitory apartment
at Haifa University with four Israeli students. I see for the
first time the contrast between Israeli and American students. For one thing, Israeli students are older. All the guys
have done three years in the Army. The women have done

two. And during their service, they have taken on tremendous responsibilities, some of them life-and-death responsibilities. They are more focused than the usual American student. They know what they want to do, and they work very hard. It's not unusual for them to do a four-year degree in three years. And whereas an American has summers off for relaxation, the Israeli male has to do his *Miluim*, his reserve army duty. On top of that, the Israeli student, unless he is very rich, has to work to earn money to pay for his education because, though tuition is subsidized and students are entitled to all sorts of discounts, they are still faced with huge expenses every year.

Throughout that semester, Steve and I study Hebrew, Israeli history, and sociology. On long weekends, the two of us take off to explore the country. We make *tiyulim*, or trips, from the Golan Heights to the Sinai. Steve is a perfect traveler, with an insatiable fund of curiosity. It is his curiosity that brought him to Israel to begin with.

A tall, soft-spoken Lutheran from Oshkosh, Wisconsin, who once studied for the ministry, he knows more about Judaism and about Israel than any of the other people in the program. He knows it not only from a historical and Biblical perspective, but also from a Christian point of view. He has one of the most open minds of anyone I have ever known, and we stay up and talk for hours, for days on end, about Zionism, particle physics, Oshkosh, and his love for his girlfriend, Cindy, who is touring Europe with a university choir. Later, he will marry Cindy, and I will be best man at their Wisconsin wedding.

Sometimes it is Steve who says, "Let's go see what the northern border looks like," and the two of us hop on a northbound bus and go. Sometimes I say, "I wonder what a Bedouin encampment is like," and off we go into the Negev. Once, we spent a weekend with the Hebrews of Dimona, a sect of Chicago blacks who are convinced that they are the only true Jews. On another occasion, we climb to the top of a mountain in the Sinai desert and spend the night there in our sleeping bags. When we wake the following morning, the air is so bright and clear we can see across the Gulf of Aqaba all the way up and down the Saudi Arabian coast. This is right before the Sinai is scheduled to be returned to Egypt as part of the Camp David accord. "You know," says Steve, who shares with me a longing to visit Egypt, "if we just sit here long enough, we can get to Egypt without moving a muscle."

One morning he says, "Let's go to Gaza."

It is in Gaza that I see, for the first time, the squalor of a Palestinian refugee camp. And also for the first time, Israeli soldiers patrolling a Palestinian area, stopping civilians to check their ID cards. But essentially, Steve and I are tourists in town—which does not prevent the local shopkeepers from voicing their complaints to us about the Israeli occupation.

We wander around the back streets until we come upon an old battered sign that says in English TURKEESH BATH. We walk down a winding staircase and under a Roman arch into a hallway where we find a reception desk. The Arab sitting behind it speaks no English. Steve and I flounder for a while with gestures trying to make ourselves understood. Then, from the interior of the bath house, a tall old black man wearing a jallabiya and a kefiyah over his shoulders emerges and takes charge of the conversation. His English is fractured; his Arabic is fluent. We learn from him that the bath house has been in continuous use since Roman times and that he is the grandson of an American soldier from Kentucky who served in Gaza with the American Expeditionary Force that had been sent there to fight the Turks during World War I. The war over, the soldier settled in Gaza because, as a black man, he felt more comfortable there than in Kentucky.

It is a wonderful, if improbable, story. A fine prelude to the Turkish bath that follows: the soaking in tepid water; the body scrub by an attendant wielding a luffa brush; the scalding tub followed by a cool bath; and the long rest on cots sipping sweet mint tea.

That Christmas, Steve and I go to Bethlehem so he can attend midnight mass at the Church of the Nativity. Watching Steve, I have some sense of how important this occasion is for a Christian. The crowds streaming through the church have come from all over the world to be in that place on that day. A single event, two thousand years ago, links them all: nuns from Namibia, pilgrims from Pennsylvania, dark-suited men from Hong Kong. Men and women from Ireland, Spain, Brazil.

And of course there is the ubiquitous Israeli soldier, in the bitter cold, in the driving rain, standing guard on the nearby roofs, stopping the pilgrims at the entrance to Manger Square to check their packages and handbags for weapons or bombs, while behind them carolers from all over the world sing "Silent Night," "Adeste Fidelis," and "It Came Upon a Midnight Clear" in a variety of languages.

Inside the church, Steve is on a real high, intent on absorbing the whole event: the priests in their embroidered robes moving down the aisles; acolytes swinging their censers; the Latin liturgy resonating from the ancient walls. Steve waits in the long line of pilgrims for his turn to take Communion.

After the mass, we hurry to the local post office, where Steve, by prearrangement, telephones his church in Oshkosh, where a loudspeaker is set up so that the members of his congregation can hear his report on Christmas Eve in Bethlehem.

In January 1982, Steve goes back to Wisconsin and to Cindy and I return to my work on the kibbutz, where I stay until

July. In June, Israel, suffering from Katyusha rocket attacks across the northern border, invades Lebanon, determined to push back the PLO.

There is not the same sense of imminent danger that was felt in 1973, and serious, painful questions would later be raised about how far the Israeli Army had gone and what had been achieved. But for now, and for the people involved, this is a war like any other.

Once again, the country's young men disappear. I am one of the few males left on my kibbutz, and suddenly the role of the volunteers takes on new meaning. We shoulder a considerable part of the burden of keeping the kibbutz going, though without us, I guess the kibbutz would get on somehow. Because productivity doesn't go down in Israel during a war. People just fill in and work harder, and with a lot more gusto. For instance, though the war breaks out in the middle of harvest time, the women bring the crops in.

At the same time, there is emotional tension everywhere. Women worry about their men, families are divided. One of the guys on the kibbutz, Itzik, a company commander in the tank corps, is among the first men to be called up. The fact that his wife is going to have a baby is not considered reason enough for the Army to send him home, so he isn't there when the baby is born on the fifth day of the war. It isn't until a week later that Itzik finally gets to see his son.

By July, the war is winding down and the men start coming home. Our kibbutz jeeps, which were requisitioned by the Army, are "discharged." The pressure on the kibbutz subsides and I decide to make that long deferred trip to Egypt. I buy a twenty-dollar ticket on the Number 100 bus that goes from Tel Aviv to Cairo. At the border crossing at Rafah, the passengers have to pass first through Israeli, then Egyptian, scrutiny. There are papers to be checked, bags inspected, money to be exchanged. Then the trip is resumed, this time on an Egyptian bus.

From here on, throughout the entire journey to the Suez Canal, one sees out of the bus window the burned-out hulks of trucks, half-tracks, and tanks, Israeli and Egyptian. These are not deliberate monuments, but still, they are grim reminders of three costly wars. When we finally cross the Canal, the signs of war disappear. After a hiatus of fifteen years, ships are plying back and forth across the waterway.

In Cairo I see all the things I once dreamed of seeing: the pyramids, the Valley of the Kings, the Nile, Memphis. On my last day in Cairo, just before my return to Israel, I share a cab to the bus station with a thirty-four-year-old Israeli. The Israeli says, "This is a special trip for me. Just last week, I finished my reserve military service on the outskirts of Beirut, got my discharge in Tel Aviv, and took right off for Cairo. Not many Israelis have made the trip, Beirut–Tel Aviv–Cairo all in one sweep."

The taxi driver turns to look at us. "So you're from Israel," he says. "Welcome."

In the conversation that follows we all agree, a bit edgily, that peace is nice. That it is a shame we had to fight so many wars. The driver says, "I served in the Egyptian Army in the October War."

"Oh, really," says the Israeli, "so did I. Where were you?"

"I was at Suez City," says the Egyptian.

"Oh really. So was I."

Suddenly, I am tense. What old hatreds are about to be stirred up?

There is a long silence. Finally, the driver and the Israeli smile and start to exchange reminiscences of the battle from their different perspectives, like a couple of Monday night quarterbacks.

The Israeli says, "Do you remember the force that flanked you from the north? Well, that was us."

"Yeah, you sure had us fooled. We were on the rooftops, expecting you to come from the south."

When we reach the bus station, the driver parks his cab, and we settle in at a café, where the two of them go on with their memories.

Back on the kibbutz I say goodbye to my friends because I have made the decision to return to San Francisco to finish my education. But I've also decided that the move is temporary. Several vague notions that have gnawed at me over the years in Israel and in Rabbi White's classes have finally come together to form a single, clear, decision. Israel is where I belong. So, though I'm leaving, I know one thing for sure. I'll be back.

San Francisco State University is the kind of school that used to be called a "streetcar college." Its students tend to be a little older than those at other four-year colleges. Most of the students, me included, support themselves by working full or part time. The student population is a mixture of social classes and racial and ethnic groups, including, to my surprise, a thousand Jews and several hundred Palestinians.

I run into young activist Palestinians when they show up to heckle speakers at Zionist activities. Curious to know who they are, I begin to attend their functions on and off campus —cultural festivals, fairs, pro-PLO rallies.

What is clear at once is their deep sense of having been wronged. That they are a nation with their own language, heritage, and culture. In their view, they have been wronged by everyone: mostly by Israel, but also by other Arabs. And they hate all those who have wronged them: their own leadership in the PLO, the Jordanians, the Syrians, the Arab League, and especially Israel.

I am taking a winter intersession course on the Middle East when I notice that one of the Arab students in the class is wearing a sweatshirt with the words BIR ZEIT UNIVERSITY stenciled on it.

"You really a student at Bir Zeit?" I ask. His name is Khalid. He's about five eight, just a little shorter than I am. His hair is black, his complexion dark, but he has bright, bright blue eyes—which, later, he will tell me the Palestinians call Crusader eyes.

"Yes. I've taken courses there. I'm at Berkeley now. Do you know where Bir Zeit is?"

"I've heard of it. Never been there, actually."

And that is the beginning. We are both smokers, but he outsmokes me three to one. We make jokes about how horrible Israeli Time cigarettes are. I offer him my Marlboros, and I take one of his Camels. He doesn't turn antagonistic when he learns that I am active in a Zionist organization, but continues to be as curious about me as I am about him. Over the course of the winter we see each other frequently. Sometimes we pass each other at demonstrations. Once, at a rally against Rabbi Meir Kahane, the extremist right-winger, Khalid is in a circle of Palestinian pickets, while I am marching in a tangential circle with anti-Kahane Zionists. Seeing each other, we nod.

One way or another, and without either of us retreating in any way from our prepared political positions, we acknowledge that a friendship is developing between us. I have to set aside my comfortable preconceptions about Arabs, and he has to do the same with his about Jews. We talk about our childhoods, about our families. He learns that I have lived on a kibbutz; I learn that he has never crossed the Green Line that separates the Occupied Territory from Israel. As a mark of his trust, he tells me his last name, then his phone number. Important concessions in the face of the rumors widely believed by Palestinians that all Zionist students are agents of Mossad, Israel's secret service.

We develop a common language because both of us are

activists. I am the chair of my organization; later, at Berkeley, he is the chair of his. We talk about organizational strategies: how to set up a phone tree, how to pick and make good use of speakers. We comment about each other's speakers. I critique his, he critiques mine.

Meanwhile I am finishing my bachelor's degree at San Francisco State. I am also in love, with Claire, the treasurer of our Zionist organization, an olive-skinned, almond-eyed psychology major with long straight black hair. We ride my bright red Yamaha 400 motorcycle up and down the coast: Santa Cruz, Carmel to the south; Tiburon, Point Reyes to the north.

I take scuba lessons and dive off Monterey. I like the quiet under water, the swaying of the kelp. I like the playfulness of the seals who come to nibble at my flippers and then, having frightened me into thinking the dark shape I saw was a shark, meet me at the surface and applaud my panicked lunge upward.

In the course of the next two years, while I am in school, I start the paperwork that will lead to Israeli citizenship. I talk to Israelis and to American immigrants and get the scoop about what stuff to bring, what stuff to ship. I fill out immigration applications and health forms; I submit twenty photographs. I quit smoking.

4

August 15, 1985

Dearest Aaron,

This is a letter out of the blue which I have finally decided to write because, though we've talked about how I feel about your decision to go to Israel, I continue to be nagged by the possibility that the full meaning of our conversations on the subject is not yet clear.

You have been clear enough. You think you must go. Your feelings and your instincts, and your own sense of self development, require you to go.

I cannot argue with you, and of course, I won't. But what I'm afraid of is that you may read just that attitude on my part as a form of affectionate lack of interest —worse, lack of care.

Much of what I have to say is not any different from what you've heard me say before: You are a grown man and you will do what you think you must. But even grown men are entitled to hear the voices of concern from people who love them.

OK. This is what I'm trying to say. I love you very much. Your decision to go to Israel, and of course, and particularly, your decision to go into the army scares me. It scares me a lot. It worries me—a lot. There is real danger in what you are going to do. I'm selfish and I'm greedy. I've seen you grow up to be a splendid man and I love having you for my son. For me the consequences are simple: I love you and I don't want to see you in danger.

And this is linked to something else that pretends to be authentic political criticism of Israel in its present moment of history but which may also be your frightened father doing what he can to keep you from going: still, I do *feel* what I'm saying, so in that sense it is true. When, in 1973, we four were in Israel and there was a war on, we all of us decided to stay, to take whatever risk there might have been (in fact, finally, there was not very much, but we couldn't have known that) because Israel was threatened from without and the risk we took had, in 1973, a kind of Jewish inevitability and authenticity about it. Post-Lebanon Israel, on the other hand, is a place that makes me queasy and I feel heartsick that the dangers you face are Shiite or West Bank terrorists, or Kahane-type Jewish violence.

When all that is said, the bottom line is that we face a paradox: this letter means to be an act of love but you may read it as a ghastly form of manipulation. There is no question that I want to manipulate—I want you not to go. But I thought, and I think, that you ought to see clearly and to hear precisely what your going will mean to me. There will never be any less love, no matter what you do.

One last thing. I have spoken throughout this letter

as if I was writing for myself alone. All the pronouns are "I" and "me." But Deborah and I have had long conversations about your going and I know she shares my hope that you'll reconsider.

There you have it, Aaron.

A letter from your father.

Be well and happy,
L.

September 2, 1985

Dear Mom and Dad,

It's taken me a long time to sit down to answer your letter but it certainly has not been far from my thoughts. I've gone through a spectrum of emotion regarding it—from perplexity to anger. I think my final response is first to thank you—you would not be the parents that I love had you held it back—but also to be a little surprised at *your* surprise at my decision.

The surprise comes because, when one looks at where I come from, my decision seems inevitable. Pop —this letter from a man who worked as a union organizer for the sake of The Revolution? Mom—this letter from a front line fighter of the Free Speech Movement? Folks—this letter from a couple who taught me, above all else, to see my convictions through to their conclusions: that the single worst sentence a person can utter begins with, "I should have . . ."? Hence, the surprise.

Dad, you wrote about this decision in the *Passion of Israel*—seventeen years ago. Logistically, this is the last chance I have to give this thing a good try. Rest assured, though, that I have the same hesitations as you and that I'm going to do this very, very, carefully.

So, for the training—thanks. For objecting—thanks.

And mostly, for supporting despite the objections—
thanks.

I love you.

A.

5

This week in the middle of basic training is called Field Training Week. Everyone has warned me that this will be the nightmare part of basic, and now, I'm in the throes of it.

We've been marched from our base camp on the beach five miles away through the sand dunes to a virgin field of thorn and thistle plants—acres of them. We're carrying all of our personal equipment plus all the equipment from the base: five-gallon jerry cans, tents, twenty-pound hammers, as well as a week's supply of food. We're staggering under the weight of our stuff when Moshe, our sergeant, shouts, "Put your loads down."

We exchange relieved looks and set down what we're carrying. Then Moshe shouts, "Now, crawl!"

I have time to think, "Is he nuts?" Then I'm on my elbows and knees. I feel the pain of a million tiny needles penetrating my uniform, puncturing my skin. Fortunately, we're wearing ammunition webbing that protects parts of our bodies from the thorns; unfortunately, the corners of the magazines in the webbing press cruelly into our ribs.

"You've got no cover! Roll to the right!" I roll and feel the thorns puncturing my sides and back.

"Now forward! Crawl!"

Hours go by in the ninety-degree heat. We do nothing but crawl. Once, when Josh, the Frenchman, tries to make his life a little easier by crawling around a particularly large and intimidating thorn bush, Sergeant Ronni picks him up by his collar and belt and grunts, "Through the thorns, Josh. Through them." And tosses him full force into the thorn bush. Later, Lieutenant Eli, our platoon commander, walks by and decides that I'm not giving my all. To encourage me, he makes me carry his full weight on my back as I crawl through the thorns. I think a few choice thoughts about overweight lieutenants.

My body thinks this whole exercise is ridiculous, but my mind, after twelve weeks of basic training, already knows that I will learn something from it. Even as I crawl, I can feel that I'm starting to move and think like a soldier. My rifle is always parallel to my line of sight; my hand is always folded over the grip, my forefinger hovering over the trigger. The equipment I've worked on—my helmet, my *ephod* fit snugly. As I look around, I begin to identify places around me from which one could expect an attack. I notice, too, the places where I would find cover in case we are attacked.

In the midst of the dust and the heat and the pain, it's hard to believe that only twelve weeks ago I was a *bizbuzz*.

Spring 1986

Home for me, once again, is Kibbutz Kfar Hamaccabi, which, when I returned to Israel in January, adopted me for the duration of my army service. The kibbutz gives me a room, and feeds me when I come back to it on my free time. It does my laundry and sends me Care packages. I have been taken in once again by the Konnellos, the kibbutz family who adopted me six years ago, and with whom I have remained in touch. As if I had never left, I pick up my friendship with their son, Ron, who is now finishing his three-year service in the Combat Engineers.

I am on the kibbutz partly in fulfillment of my assignment as a Nahal soldier. Nahal, an acronym of *Noar Halutz Lohem,* Fighting Pioneer Youth, was established in 1950 by David Ben Gurion, Israel's first prime minister, as a way of giving soldiers both military skill and pioneering capabilities. Initially, everyone in the army put in six months on an agricultural settlement as part of his military service. Now, Nahal is an integral branch of the infantry but service in it is voluntary. As a Nahal infantryman, my service will include six months of work on the kibbutz, six months of basic training, including language instruction, six months in the Nahal Brigade, and finally, six months in the Nahal battalion of the Paratroop Brigade.

On the kibbutz the work committee asks me to choose between the tire retread factory and the cow barn. In a burst of candor, they tell me that Eli, who is in charge of the cow barn, isn't enthusiastic about having Americans working for him. "However," says one of the committee, "if you've had any experience with cows, he might be persuaded to let you work there."

"As it happens," I say, "I have had some experience with cows."

I was on my second voyage in the Merchant Marines, on a vessel bound from Seattle to Kobe, Japan. Our cargo included twenty head of steer crammed, five steers together, into four twenty-foot containers on the afterdeck behind the wheelhouse. The cows were supposed to be looked after by a man named Bill, a stocky forty-year-old cowboy from Seattle who actually sported cowboy boots, a bandanna, and a ten-gallon hat. Once at sea, Bill found the twenty steers too much to handle by himself so he asked for volunteers from the crew. Intrigued, I volunteered.

They were heavy creatures, crammed into a small space on a boat being rocked by great ocean swells. It was not long before they were seasick, spewing at both ends and utterly ignoring the bales of hay which, once a day, I dropped into their containers.

One night I sat on a bale drinking beer with a sailor from Arkansas and another from Massachusetts. The moon laid down a long line of yellow light off to starboard. Our mood was very mellow, when the seasick steers in the containers below us set up their unhappy bellowing. "Moooo," they moaned, and as the rocking of the ship increased their distress, "Mooooo," they cried again.

Of course I've got experience . . .

February 1986

Dear Folks (or as we cowboys say, Shalom),
Yes, cows. Six days a week, eight hours a day. Up to my knees, up to my elbows in cow(s). Ask me and I'll tell you about milking, shots, milking, herding, milking, births, and milking. Three hundred Holsteins, milked three times a day.

Cows!

It's strange being back on the kibbutz after four years. Much has changed, but in some ways nothing has really changed. The kibbutz powers that be finally got concerned about the lack of young people ("youthies" as you would call them, Pop) and have made a concerted effort, including newspaper ads, to bring the median age down from sixty-three, so there are some new faces (No, I'm not getting married). But the old affection is still here. It's almost as if I had never left the kibbutz.

About the army. It looks like basic will start in July, so after that it's "Private son" to you. Also, you're not likely to hear much from me after that, but please keep your letters coming.

Recommendations for a Care package: NO DAIRY PRODUCTS. OK, maybe a little chocolate. Juicy Fruit gum, M & M's, Snickers bars. *Playboy* magazine. Also, there's no sci-fi here. See if you can find Niven's *Mote in God's Eye* or Bester's *Demolished Man*.

Oh, yes, cassettes. UB40's *Labor of Love,* or anything by John Cougar Mellenkamp. I know, such frivolity, but when you're fulfilling the collective dream of your nation and the weight of five thousand years of history is on your shoulders, you need a little background music.

Also, send *Spider-Man* comics.

Know that I love you and I feel good.

A.

As the months pass, the weather warms up. When the rainy season ends, it turns out to be much pleasanter milking dry cows than wet ones. The days grow longer, and when I am finished with the cows, I take long horseback rides through the sprouting wheatfields. I check: the Israeli Army has no cavalry. On weekends, I occasionally scuba dive among the submerged Crusader ruins off the Acco coast, but visibility is usually poor and the water teems with giant Medusas, stinging jellyfish.

On February 22, Natan Scharansky arrives in Israel, freed from a Soviet prison in which he spent fourteen years. The absolute symbol of resistance to Soviet oppression, he is hailed as a hero by thousands of people at the airport. Everyone feels the poignancy of his meeting with his wife, whom he has not seen since his imprisonment.

On March 8, John Demjanjuk, known as Ivan the Terrible to his victims, is extradited from Cleveland, Ohio, and brought to Israel, where he will be tried and convicted for killing hundreds of Jews and Ukrainians in the Treblinka concentration camp during World War II.

In April, the Israeli Supreme Court forces Itzhak Peretz, the Interior Minister, to introduce Daylight Saving Time, a move Peretz, an Orthodox Jew, resisted because he feared it would encourage violation of the Sabbath.

In May, the headlines talk of war with Syria.

At intervals, I go off to the Induction Center in Haifa, where I am given a barrage of tests: psycho-technic, language, and physical. My "profile," that is, the number that indicates my degree of fitness, is 97. In American draft lingo, I am 1A. More than that—I qualify for a combat unit.

I also attend a seminar sponsored by the Kibbutz movement, at which I meet other immigrants with whom I will be inducted into the Army. Nahal encourages friends or schoolmates, and especially people from the same youth movement, to be inducted together in groups that are called *garinim* (the word *garin* means seed, and the implication is that from these seeds, settlements will grow). Since new immigrants don't have such affiliations, we will form a *garin* of newcomers. The immigration experience is what we will have in common, and we choose a name, "Garin Pezer," to reflect that fact. *Pezer* is the Hebrew root of the word *mefuzar*, "spread out," referring both to our various origins and to the fact that, unlike Israeli-born *garinim*, we live on several kibbutzim.

All of us are apprehensive and pelt our instructors with questions which we hope will produce reassuring answers. "How many pairs of underwear will we be issued in winter, and what happens if they get wet?" The reply, "Two, and too damned bad," is not reassuring. The South Africans and the Americans worry about having to serve on the West Bank: will we be there, if so for how long, and what will we be expected to do? But there are no straightforward replies —not because anyone is hiding information. It's just that nobody really knows the answers. Our biggest, most overriding, question is how hard physically will our training be? The answer is, "Hard. Even very hard. But *gam ze ya'avor*, that too will pass."

It is at this seminar that I meet Jake from New York; David from New Jersey; Nathan and Bill, both from Washington D.C.; and Alan from Chicago. There is also a group of four guys from South Africa, who are all on the same kibbutz. Others include the Englishman Tommy, Manny from Argentina, Mario from Italy, and Danno from Australia.

Most of these guys have come to Israel without their families and they have come for all sorts of reasons. There are ideologues among them who want to be part of the Zionist "ingathering of the exiles." Others are here to escape political persecution. Still others, driven by personal restlessness, are in Israel simply because it is one more new place to be. In this group, some want to be in the Army. The rest of us simply want to become Israelis. But you can't do one without the other.

July 1986

I'm in line at the induction center, "somewhere in the middle of the country." I showed up this morning at a collection point in Haifa, where I joined a group of draftees. We were loaded on to a bus that brought us here.

The Army has this down to a science. I move from cubicle to cubicle. Some guy opens my mouth and checks my teeth. In the next cubicle I get a tetanus shot. In the one after that I fill out a form on which I designate my next of kin. Then I sign a form that gives the government permission to deduct eighteen *agurot* (about twelve cents) from my monthly pay.

"For what?"

"Life insurance."

Then I get a little POW card imprinted with excerpts from the Geneva Convention. Inside is my name, rank, serial number, and blood type—something neat to hand my captors in case I am ever taken prisoner. I also get a dog tag. It's made so it can be broken in two.

"Why?" I ask.

"Just for good bookkeeping. If you're killed, one stays on your body, and the other gets sent to Central Command."

"Oh," I say.

"Here," he says, as he hands me an additional pair of dog tags that fit into little pockets sewn into each of my boots.

"What are these for?"

The sergeant, who has answered questions like mine a thousand times, is patient. "In case the ones around your neck are shot away, and you turn out to be unrecognizable. Be glad, soldier. Your Army thinks of everything."

"Thanks," I say.

The Army continues to think of everything when I follow to the barber those of my group who need their hair cut. He doesn't exactly scalp the guys, but their hair is left very short. Not Marine Corps short, but short enough so that if some enemy wants to grab the hair on the back of your neck, he won't find a handhold.

Farther down the line, I am given olive drab underwear by a thin, stylish corporal with neatly parted hair, who casually looks me up and down and then throws me two pairs of shiny red boots, two pairs of pants, three shirts, and a jacket —my dress uniform. To my surprise, when I try them on, they all fit perfectly. Then we are told to go home for a week. "Be at your base a week from Sunday, eight o'clock sharp. Dismissed."

I look around. All of us are trying to feel comfortable in

the new uniforms, and it's just as obvious that we aren't. The
shoes are so new, they squeak when we walk. The shirts and
trousers have razor-sharp creases. We look, in a word, pretty.
And we can already anticipate what will happen the minute
we're seen out in the real world. *"Bizbuzz, bizbuzz."* It's the
name Israelis give to what happens when guys like us are
seen walking along in our brand-new crisp uniforms, without
insignia. *"Bzzzzzz, bzzzzz."* It's a sound that follows the
new soldier. Since practically everyone has been or will be in
the army, it's an amused, and affectionate, sound of recognition. A form of encouragement, of sympathy for what we're
going through, but it also conveys a tongue-in-cheek mock-
ery. As we pass through the gates of the induction center, we
cringe as it begins. *"Bzzzzz, bzzzzz. Bzzzzzz, bzzzzzz."*

I'm in the Army now.

It's hard to recognize the civilians we were in this group of
guys with their short haircuts, their neatly pressed green
uniforms, and new boots. We leave the induction center bid-
ding farewell to each other, and go off to our various kibbutzim. We will meet again a week from now at our Nahal
training base. I barely hear the "buzzing" being directed at
me on my way home because I am concentrating so hard on
memorizing my new serial number.

Later, I will complain to my kibbutz brother, Ron, that it's
better to be a civilian than a soldier. "Yes," he will correct
me, "but the best is being a soldier on vacation." I appreciate that feeling now as I head into the kibbutz, jaunty in my
new uniform. No cows to milk and, as yet, no thorns to crawl
through.

Ron shakes his head in dismay at the straight creases in
my pants, the bright red shine of my boots. "You *bizbuzz*. It
looks like it's up to me to make you look like a soldier."

Although he is three years my junior, Ron now takes the
role of a veteran helping his kid brother into the Army. He

throws my uniform straight into the laundry, the first of four washings it will see this week. He shows me how to oil my boots and break them in so I will get fewer blisters. He laminates my POW card and waterproofs my field dressing, both of which I have to carry from now on. He "night-proofs" my dog tags, covering the chain with a black shoelace and the tags with cloth so they won't flash at night. And he gets me an army green watchcover for the same reason. "There," he says, when he is done. "That ought to put you ahead in basic. You might even catch some free time."

My last week of freedom passes peacefully. For me, not for the Army. On July 19, four terrorists in a dinghy are spotted in the predawn hours ten kilometers north of Nahariya, just at the northern border. In the clash that follows two Israeli soldiers are killed and nine wounded. All four terrorists are killed.

I notice that I am noticing this kind of thing in the news.

In the meantime, my lessons with Ron continue. He shows me how to tie my shoelaces so the medics can cut right through them if they should have to. We take out his Galil assault rifle and I learn to field-strip it—first in daylight, then in darkness, and finally blindfolded. I'm good, but slow. Arlene, a kibbutz volunteer from Washington, D.C., who is sitting in on the lessons, beats me every time.

Finally, on Saturday evening, the day before I'm due to report, Ron comes by my room with two presents. "Here, this is a loan for the next year and a half." It's his gunstrap, custom-made from the seat belt of an abandoned car in Lebanon. It is wider and more comfortable than the one I will be issued. "And"—he looks sheepish—"this you can have." It's a small card on which is printed the *Tfillat Haderech*, the "Prayer for a Journey," on one side, and the *Tfillah Lifnai Krav*, the "Prayer Before Going into Combat," on the other.

"Not that I believe in it or anything," he mumbles.

I smile. The prayer card, too, has been laminated in plastic.

August 1986

Dear Folks,

Just a quick note to let you know all's well. I'm working hard but surviving. The ulpan [language course] is very intense, so I learn a lot. Our commanders seem to know what they're doing and the food is OK. Also, Mom, we haven't left the training base and aren't likely to for a while. It's in the middle of the country and safe, oh so safe . . .

So please don't worry. I'm tired but I feel good. Lots of love,

A.

I walk into the Nahal Training Base for the first time. I try to look casual as I pass the base guard, as if I've walked into hundreds of army bases and am just checking this one out for comparison. The guard sees right through me and points me to where my *garin* members are sitting. As I join Nathan and Jake I notice with satisfaction that their uniforms aren't quite as worn in as mine.

We sit by the side of the obstacle course waiting for it to be 8 A.M., 0800, the time we were told to report. Each of us has what is called the *kitbeg aleph*, a barracks bag now lightly filled with the dress clothes we received at the induction center. I look around trying to think of anything but what lies ahead. I already know it's going to involve shouting and running and pain.

Our base, built by the British in pre-state Palestine, was taken over by the new Israeli Army in 1948. It's what's called a "permanent base," which means that, in addition to the tents in which the men are quartered, there are also some concrete buildings: the dining hall, the PX, the sergeants' and officers' quarters. We trainees will get to see only the dining hall.

The base sergeant, Banai, a short, stocky Yemenite with a handlebar moustache, is legendary throughout Israel. Anybody who has served in Nahal knows him, and a great many others who haven't. And it is due to his efforts that the base isn't a crumbling ruin.

Banai is strict. He has been known to punish sergeants, and even officers, who come under his command in matters relating to camp discipline, for minor infringements of the rules: wrongly tied shoelaces, going without a cap. And he is especially fierce about maintaining the base grounds and equipment. For instance, though there are scores of eucalyptus trees growing in the sandy soil of the base, one never sees traces of sand or stray leaves on the walkways. Banai lore has it that he knows when a leaf is about to fall and sends a trainee to catch it before it hits the ground. Fortunately for us, he has a soft spot in his heart for new immigrants.

At 0800 precisely we hear a whipcrack shout, "On your feet, *ta'amdu beshloshot,* stand in threes. Get those *kitbegim* up. Not over your right shoulder . . . that's for your gun."

Since we haven't been issued a gun yet, I say, "Excuse me."

"Excuse me," he snaps. "There's no 'Excuse me' in the Army. What am I, your friend?"

This is Sergeant Moshe. He is a tall, lean Turk whose coal black eyes seem to rage with fire. But every so often that fire subsides to a gleaming spark of humor, which makes us suspect that his anger is mostly theatrical. At least we hope so.

He turns his attention to Josh. "Hey, soldier, back off.

Whoever told you you could stand closer than six feet from a commander? You want to jump into my bed, too?"

We march to the auditorium herded by Sergeant Moshe's invectives. *"Smoll, yamin, smoll,* left, right, left. No, dammit, soldier, your other left! And what the hell is the matter with *you,* did you lose something? No? Then keep your head high and your eyes straight or I'll take your head off myself."

Finally, he lines us up single file outside the entrance to the auditorium. And now Sergeant Moshe teaches us to salute: "From the shoulder to the elbow out from your body and horizontal to the ground, hand brought up straight and at a forty-five-degree angle along the side of your face."

In his zeal Sergeant Moshe adds a particularly dainty bend at the waist. Nobody laughs. He explains, or rather shouts, that we are about to meet our platoon commander. "Remember, stand six feet from his desk and salute. Then answer his questions and only his questions. Keep your replies short, concise. Follow every answer with 'sir' and salute as you leave. Is that clear?"

"Yeah, sure, fine."

"Mah zeh? What's that? When you talk to me you say, 'Yes, sir,' loudly and in unison. That sloppiness will cost you. I won't forget it, is that clear?"

"Yes, sir!!" we shout, loudly and in unison.

The irony of all that bluster is that the Israeli Army is one of the least rank-conscious military services in the world. Evolving as it has out of the socialist-influenced underground armies of pre-state days, it has never stressed spit and polish discipline for its own sake. And since every officer makes his way through the ranks, and has a very clear understanding of what it is like to be an enlisted man, there is no great social gap between him and his men.

In addition to that, an Israeli officer is bound by the very famous *"Acharai,* follow me!" code. The point is that, both in training and in combat, the officer is expected to *lead* his men, to be, in the most literal sense, in front of them, as well as to exemplify the best qualities of soldiering. A man who will one day in combat shout, "After me, boys, let's take that hill" does not treat his men as inferiors.

So now, at the very beginning of basic training, I know that all this bluster about discipline is only temporary; that by the end of basic I will be calling my commanders by their first names and discussing orders. I will actually forget how to salute. For the time being, though, we are being trained to obey orders *to the letter*. It doesn't matter if we understand the reason for an order, we are required to obey it. And failure to obey orders will get the individual soldier, and frequently the whole unit, into trouble. For now, as I wait my turn to meet our commander, I practice my salute, trying especially hard to hold my hand at the proper angle to my face. I make four practice salutes when suddenly it's my turn to stand before Second Lieutenant Eli.

Six feet back. Stand straight, salute.

"Name and serial number?"

"Wolf, Aaron, 4383831, sir!" Except for that bar up on his shoulders, he doesn't look like anything special.

"Are you ready for some hard work?"

"Yes, sir." Do I have a choice? Do I get to say, "No, sir, I'd like to sit out the next six months under the shade of a cork tree smelling the flowers"? I do not. I get to say, "Yes, sir."

"Dismissed," he says, and I salute.

Is that it? This tubby fellow with the shiny blue eyes is the Israeli Army's version of a hotshot commanding officer?

It won't be long before this soft-looking guy will be running us all right into the ground.

The next six weeks are pre-basic training. We are the only platoon on the base, and we are put through a program especially designed for new immigrants to help us overcome our language and cultural disabilities. The sabras, who will be joining us later, have certain advantages over us.

For one thing, they are native Hebrew speakers. For another, they have grown up expecting to be in the Army. They have brothers and fathers and mothers and sisters and uncles and aunts who have been in the Army, and that helps prepare them psychologically for what they're going to go through. We immigrants don't have any of that, and this six-week period in which we are kept together is meant to lessen the gap between us and the sabras. We'll spend eight hours a day in language study. The rest of the day will be devoted to military matters: discipline, equipment, and physical training.

The discipline begins at once as Sergeant Moshe, who has lined us up again, barks, "We have an account to settle. From now on, you'll remember to say 'sir' when you talk to me. Around the auditorium, thirty seconds, move!"

We do not hesitate. We move.

There are all sorts of punishments for infractions of the rules. "Do twenty push-ups, now!" "Do forty push-ups, now!" But the typical punishment is running.

Usually we're punished for carelessness about time. The art of being on time is given special consideration in basic training so that we will have the habit of precision when we receive orders like, "Give us three minutes of cover fire, then flank right and meet us at eighteen thirty-two."

For instance, we'll be called out for morning roll call and some sleepy head is four seconds late. Or we don't get our tents in order in the seven allotted minutes. Or we take longer than three minutes to get ready to eat. Or we take more than nineteen minutes to eat. "OK," Sergeant Ronni says, "give me thirty seconds, around the bathroom. *Zuz*, move!" Now the bathroom is thirty yards away, so we really

have to move it. We run like hell, get back, and line up in
perfect formation.

"Too bad," the sergeant says. "Two seconds late. Thirty
seconds, around the bathroom, *zuz.*" And off we go. Sometimes this series of circuits around the bathroom can last an
hour and a half.

For more serious punishment, we are made to run carrying weight. "OK," the sergeant will say. "You've done it
three times and you still can't get it right. Now, fall out and
get your *kitbegim.*" So we do, and off we go, running again.
If we still aren't doing it right, we are made to carry all kinds
of loads: filled five-gallon jerry cans, fifty-gallon (empty) barrels, or even a man on a stretcher. Though this is rare,
because the Army doesn't want us to associate the life-saving
task of carrying a man on a stretcher with punishment.

A frequent punishment is called the "about-face-jump."
That happens in the midst of some activity when the sergeant decides we've goofed. Marching out of step, for example. Without warning, he shouts, *"Le'achor kfotz!* About face,
jump!" And there we are, some forty guys, twenty-four or
twenty-five years old, some of us with degrees in Russian
literature or Phi Beta Kappa keys, leaping into the air and
turning a hundred and eighty degrees before we hit the
ground, and doing it ten, fifty, or a hundred times in a row
all because some nineteen-year-old Israeli who has three
stripes on his sleeve calls out, "About face, jump." It is a
perfectly ludicrous punishment because it is so absolutely
pointless. And maybe that's the point.

Even about-face-jump, however, can have its comic side.
When Alex, one of our South Africans, who is also a world-
class gymnast, is punished with the command, he executes a
perfect backflip and lands on his feet. He does it so well that
Sergeant Ronni, who loves watching him do it, comes close
to picking on him just to see him jump.

These punishments are comparatively easy to put up with.

They can be shrugged off and forgotten. What really hurts is
when one of us has time deducted from the weekend pass to
which we are entitled once every two or three weeks. A
soldier who has broken some really serious rule can be punished by having to stay in camp for an extra hour or more on
Friday evening when all of us are panting to go home. The
delay itself is bad enough, but in addition to that you end up
missing the bus you need.

But the worst, the absolute worst, punishment (this side of
actually being sent to jail) is to have your entire Saturday
leave of absence canceled. Because, oh how we look forward
to going home. We count the hours, the days, the weeks from
one weekend pass to the next. So your heart really sinks
when you hear the word *Shabbat* coming at you. A word that
you usually associate with the peace of the Sabbath fills you
now with despair when your sergeant snaps it at you because
you've goofed up in some way. It means you stay on the base
over the weekend. It means standing extra guard time instead of seeing your parents; or working in the kitchen
scouring pots instead of going on a picnic with your girlfriend.

For the sabra soldiers who will be coming later, this punishment will prove especially hard. In general, they have a
harder time in the first few weeks of training because they're
so young—eighteen or nineteen. Many of them have never
been away from home before. And there they are being
physically and mentally tested every day. As they see it,
nobody's being nice to them and they are constantly being
yelled at for the least little thing. They do their best, and
eventually they settle down, but in those first weeks, they're
the ones who have nightmares and who start up out of their
sleep screaming for their mothers.

Take the case of Binyamin. The poor kid was the first guy
in our platoon to have "Shabbat" shouted at him by Sergeant Moshe. And when he yells out "Shabbat," it is almost

as if we are seeing a scene directed by Steven Spielberg.
Moshe puts his hand out, points at the culprit, and then
flings the dreaded word with so much unrepressed fury that
you expect the clouds to open and lightning to strike.

And it almost does when he shouts his terrible shout at
Binyamin. The kid had waked up in the night, and instead of
going to the camp toilet a couple hundred yards away, he
just peed a little distance from the tent. Sergeant Ronni saw
him and fell on him hard.

"Where the hell do you think you are? What do you think
you're doing? That's disgusting. That's revolting. What
makes you think anybody wants to live in your rotten piss?
Now you just report yourself to Moshe in the morning and
tell him what you did."

What Binyamin did isn't nice, but it's not the kind of
thing anyone would take too seriously. Normally, Moshe
would have ordered him to clean the latrines or spend a
couple of hours in the kitchen scouring pots. But Binyamin
didn't report to Moshe that morning. I don't know why.
Maybe he thought if he did nothing, his trouble would go
away.

And that was why Moshe pointed at Binyamin and roared
"Shabbat!"

"Get it straight," Moshe says, turning to us where we
stand in formation. "He's losing his *Shabbat* not because he
pissed beside the tent, but because he didn't report what he
did as he was ordered to. Is that clear?" he says, standing in
front of Binyamin.

"Clear, sir," says Binyamin in a tiny voice, as the rest of
us can see him visibly shrinking.

We fall into our pre-basic training routine. After morning
inspection we go to language class. There, for eight hours
each day, we escape Moshe and Ronni's wrath in comfortable classrooms where we are taught by soldiers who serve

in the Army's Education Branch. The Education Branch, largely made up of women, is one of the best branches of service in the Army and is charged with bringing up to an acceptable level the education of every soldier. In addition to making Hebrew speakers out of immigrants, the Education Branch works with illiterate or disadvantaged soldiers of all kinds, including former prisoners. In addition to teaching us Hebrew, the soldiers also instruct us in Israeli sociology, politics, geography, and environmental issues. Every time we go on a training mission to a new area, we're pulled aside for an hour or two by a woman who tells us about the wildlife in the area, what the trees are like, where we are in relation to the Syrio-African rift, and how that force affects the hills that we've been running up and down all morning.

As in other parts of the world, secretarial work is what women in the Israeli Army are most frequently given to do. Not all of them, however. In the Intelligence units they are the decoders, radar monitors, and language specialists. They are the ever-present military censors who interrupt your conversation on a base telephone when you have inadvertently begun to tell your girlfriend what next week's training plans are. "Sorry, soldier," she says sweetly, "you can't talk about that."

Though women are not permitted to go into combat, they can teach weaponry or tactics in combat units. There are women in the Medical Corps who serve as medics. There are even women in the Paratroop Brigade, where they are parachute packers. Because they take the entire parachute training course, it is not unusual to see them wearing the prestigious Master Jump Wings, with a star that signifies they have done fifty jumps or more.

Though our instructors are earthbound, they are endlessly imaginative. They teach us hard-to-remember Hebrew words by putting them into the context of popular songs. In a class in which we learn the Hebrew names of our equipment,

Tami, who is a Russian immigrant herself, creates an alphabetical mnemonic that helps us remember a bewildering number of new words. None of us, until now, have had much occasion to use the Hebrew word for "firing chamber" in conversation.

After our eight hours of classwork, we change to shorts and tennis shoes and go out to the exercise field for a *madas,* a sports session. Our *madasnikit,* our sports instructor, too, is a woman. Daphna is nineteen years old. She is five foot two and has long chestnut hair that she keeps tied in a ponytail. She wears a crisp white T-shirt and blue sweat pants. She is the one who makes us do push-ups, sit-ups, pull-ups. She leads us in laps around the track and through the obstacle course. She shows us the best way to climb the eight-foot wall; how to pull ourselves up on the ropes; how to hold our guns as we crawl under barbed wire. Like our language instructors, she is an ingenious teacher who invents exercises and games that will help us build up our stamina and our different muscle groups. With her sweet smile and gentle words of encouragement, we don't notice how ragged she is running us. Though she, too, is a sergeant, there is no doubt that we enjoy being with her more than we do with Moshe.

The rest of the day and part of the night is spent on real army stuff. In this first week, we are issued fatigue uniforms and a slew of equipment: a sleeping bag, two canteens, and an entrenching tool. We also get a ground cloth, tentpoles and stakes, and a mess kit that includes two sets of eating implements, one set for meat dishes, and one for dairy. This is, after all, a kosher army.

Some of our equipment needs to be modified and personalized. The helmet, for example, has to be covered in camouflage cloth and the chin strap has to be resewn to make it snug but not tight. Our ammunition webbing has to be reinforced with wire and adjusted to fit our bodies. That done, we have to waterproof our POW cards and personal bandages and "night-proof" our dog tags.

But of course, with the help of Ron, my kibbutz brother, I have already taken care of that chore, which is why I am sitting on my bunk reading today's *Ma'ariv* while everyone else in the tent is fumbling with dog tags, shoelaces, and bandages.

Just then, in walks Sergeant Moshe.

"So," he says sweetly, "I see you've got a little spare time."

"Yes, sir," I say, looking over the top of my newspaper.

"I take it you've finished with your work."

"Well, yes sir." He picks up my night-proofed dog tags, looks at my plastic-wrapped bandages and POW card.

"Nice," he says, "really nice. So you're finished?" And here his voice drops half a register.

"Yes, sir . . ."

"And your friends," he says, waving a hand to indicate the other guys on their knees wrapping plastic and dyeing shoelaces, "are they finished, too?"

"Well, no . . ."

Then boom! The *Ma'ariv* explodes as I feel myself hauled to my feet.

" 'Well, no,' is it? Listen, Wolf, you're an immigrant, so I'll teach you a new word in Hebrew. Its *sociomat*. You know what it means? It means a soldier who only takes care of himself. Is that you, Wolf? Hell, man. *Eleh hachaverim shelchah,* these guys are your friends. And this is an Army unit, dammit. And as long as one person isn't ready, the unit's not ready. So, you get in there and work.

"Oh yes," he adds, "I want to tell you one thing more. I'll be coming by later to make personally sure that you're the last guy working in the tent. Understood?"

"Yes, sir."
Understood.

In the second week of pre-basic, we are issued rifles. Though
we will be trained in their use, the weapons are not yet
technically ours. That will only happen ten weeks from now
when we are sworn into the Army at a ceremony at the
Western Wall.

The weapon is a Galil assault rifle, modeled on the Russian AK-47 and improved by the Israelis. Its safety catch
can be manipulated with either a thumb or a forefinger. It
has night sights that the AK-47 doesn't have. And it is
equipped with a bipod which has three important uses. The
obvious one is that it provides stability when shooting in a
prone position. Also, it functions as a wire clipper. But best
of all, the bipod makes a marvelous bottle opener.

I am trained to know that rifle from the inside out and
back again. I am taught to keep it cleaner than anything I've
ever owned in my life: cleaner than my motorcycle or my
teeth or my room. It is drilled into me over and over again
that keeping my Galil clean will save my life.

I develop a relationship with that gun more intimate than
I have ever had with anything. It is at my side or slung over
my shoulder all the time. I clean and oil it every night, and
wipe it clean in the morning. When I crawl into my sleeping
bag, its strap is wrapped around my wrist or around my leg.

Though the Galil is not particularly fast, it's a good, tough
gun. In my time in the Army I will wade through mud and
tramp through seawater with it, but no matter how I abuse it,
it will always be ready to fire a full thirty-five-round clip
without jamming.

But having a gun involves more than understanding how
to use it. There is an ethic in the Israeli Army called "the
purity of arms," *tohar haneshek.* It's an idea we hear about
frequently in lectures from our commanders, who make the

point that a gun is something more than just a means for
defense. There is power in a gun. And attached to power is
responsibility, because anyone who has a gun acquires some
of God's power. The power to take a life. And that means
that we have to be very careful about when we use the gun;
careful to beware of hubris.

The purity of arms is the moral guideline for behavior in
the Israeli Army. Its emphasis is on restraint, on compassion, and its bias is in favor of human life. Soldiers who loot
or who mistreat prisoners or civilians violate the idea. It was
the "purity of arms" that caused Israeli commanders in the
war in Lebanon to halt their advance to round up thirteen-
and fourteen-year-olds armed with rocket-propelled grenades
instead of shooting at them.

An ethic, then, only has meaning in action, and the burden of the purity of arms rests on each individual soldier. To
make the idea clear, each of us, when he is sworn in at the
Western Wall, will receive his weapon with one hand and a
Bible with the other.

Next to his gun, the most important tool an infantryman has
are his feet. So the Army sends us on endless marches.
Often we are rewarded with some privilege. The very first
march that we do is for the right to wear a gun strap. We
start out carrying the gun in our hands, not strapped to our
shoulders. It's a short march, maybe three miles.

We march to earn the right to wear the Nahal tag on our
shoulder. There's another march for the privilege of wearing
the infantry symbol on our green berets. At the end of basic
training we will march forty-five miles for the right to wear
the black beret. There's even a march that gives us the right
to call our commanders by their first names. We'll do short,
fast marches and long, steady ones. We'll carry a variety of
loads, from full pack and gear to jerry cans or field radios or
guys on stretchers. The longest march I'll ever do will be the

fifty-five-mile march to Jerusalem for my paratrooper's red
beret. But that's still a year down the road.

When seven weeks into our training the sabras arrive, the
pace of our military training accelerates. We immigrants say
goodbye to our Hebrew teachers and the cool classrooms
where we sat out the heat of the day. Now, Lieutenant Eli is
our teacher as we embark on a whirlwind course on the arts
of war.

For the first several weeks, we learn the theory behind
and the use of the light weaponry with which our platoon
will be equipped. We learn about the FN MAG machine gun,
the rocket-fired grenade, the rocket-propelled grenade, the
LAW antitank weapon, the 52-millimeter mortar, and the
M203 grenade launcher. We learn about grenades—antipersonnel grenades, fragmentation grenades, shock grenades,
smoke grenades, and something called exploding smoke grenades. We learn about Uzis, and M16s, and Kalachnikovs.

We also learn a little first aid.

During these lessons, we develop a symbiotic relationship
with the sabras. They help us with our Hebrew and we help
them get by.

Then, for several weeks, we leave our base with its indoor
dining hall and twelve-man tents with cement floors and start
our field training. We learn how to pitch a two-man tent, and
how to shave with the water from our canteens. We break out
our *messtingim,* our mess kits, and our two sets of silverware,
and are introduced to *manot krav,* field rations.

Every box of *manot krav* has enough food for five soldiers
for a period of twenty-four hours. Each box comes with its
own can opener, tea bags, books of matches, and packets of
salt and pepper. And each meal, whether breakfast, lunch,
or supper, is a potpourri of multinational garbage. There are
the raw chickpeas and the oily halva of the Middle Eastern
cuisine. The Bully beef and gristle chunks inherited from

the British Army. The turkey bits may be American, but if so, they are leftovers from the Civil War. Then there are the candies, of no known nationality, which can neither be sucked nor chewed and which hover in an indeterminate state between solid and liquid. Any soldier facing a diet of *manot krav* settles down for a long siege of hunger.

Here, in the field, the pace of instruction and the length of our days increase. We're on the go for eighteen to twenty hours a day. We spend most of that time on the firing range. I feel the difference between the kick of a 5.56-millimeter Galil shell and a 7.62-millimeter Kalachnikov. Then there's the FN MAG, a belt-fed machine gun that can spew a rapid and ruthless stream of 7.62-millimeter shells for as long as you can hold your finger on the trigger. To keep its barrel from bending, the gunner, who carries a spare, has to replace the overheated barrel after a thousand rounds or so.

I like shooting these weapons, and I'm an OK shot, but I particularly enjoy shooting the bigger stuff. The rocket-fired grenade, the rocket-propelled grenade, the LAW antitank weapon satisfy my hidden small boy's pleasure in a big bang. It's uncomfortably pleasing to press a button or a trigger *here* and watch a fifty-gallon drum blow up a hundred yards away.

Then there's the drama of throwing a hand grenade for the first time. I wait in line. When it's my turn, one of the sergeants hands me a flak jacket and signs a grenade out to me. Then I walk to the retaining wall, where the instructor waits. Looking over the three-foot-high wall, I can see a fifty-gallon drum some thirty feet away. The instructor says, "Pull the pin and throw it away, soldier."

I pull the pin, throw the pin away, and stand there holding the now armed grenade, my forefinger pressed against the firing mechanism.

"There now," he says. "You see how easy it is. How safe you are. By the way, how's your training coming? Been getting a little rough lately . . ." He goes on, prattling away, as if we had nothing better to do. I hold the grenade.

He's doing this deliberately. He wants me to know that I'm safe just as long as I don't take my hand away from the grenade's firing mechanism. He wants me to know I'm really safe holding a live grenade. What seems like hours later, he gets around to, "Well, soldier, what do you think? Do you want to throw that grenade, or what?"

My lips dry, I manage to say, "I want to throw it, sir."

"All right then. Remember, throw it like you would a stone. Then yell '*Rimon!* Grenade!' Watch where it lands, then duck. Got it?"

I nod. "Now, throw," he says, and I do.

Just as we're adjusting to the routine at the base camp, we get the order to break camp and load everything up on our backs. We're going to do a five-mile march to begin what is called Field Training Week . . .

After two days of crawling through thorns, we've gotten pretty good at it and are ready to move on. We do. We learn how to dig a foxhole and how to fill it up again. We learn the basics of camouflage and how to move quietly at night. We learn how to get along without eating or sleeping. Finally, we learn "intelligence-gathering techniques."

We're on the side of a low, sandy hill. It's two o'clock in the afternoon. The day is cloudless and hot. Each of us has dug a shallow trench and camouflaged it and ourselves with shrubs and twigs. I'm in full gear and helmet, lying on my gun looking downslope, so the blood rushes to my head. We are watching enemy positions and our orders are to keep a detailed log of what we see and when we see it. The enemy looks suspiciously like our Platoon 2, which is watching us and taking notes. The exercise is excruciatingly boring and I want to doze, but I know that Sergeant Moshe is prowling around carrying a big stick to poke sleepers awake. Just the same I feel myself drifting off. Then I hear the crunch of footsteps behind me and I shake myself. There is Moshe looming above me and Lieutenant Eli is with him. Moshe does all the talking.

"How you doing, Wolf?" he asks. They look down at me sternly.

"I'm awake, sir," I answer hurriedly.

"Yes, I can see that. But how do you feel?"

"Fine, sir." I wonder what I've done wrong.

"Fine, sir," he mocks. "What do you mean 'Fine, sir'? Look at you. You're lying in a dirt hole, you're covered with brambles, and you're half dead from lack of sleep. Don't give me that 'Fine, sir' crap, Wolf. What a hell of a way to celebrate."

"Celebrate, sir? I don't get it." I really don't.

Eli smiles and Moshe winks. "Happy birthday, Aaron."

It's my twenty-sixth birthday and the end of our eleventh week of training. Next week at the Western Wall we will be officially sworn into the Army. Today is also the day before Rosh Hashanah, the last day of the year 5746. It is because of Rosh Hashanah that we are about to be given our first active duty as soldiers.

This very afternoon, our entire platoon is dispersed in clusters of two or three men to Jewish settlements on the West Bank where, for the weekend, we are to take the place of reservists, older family men whom the Army wants to send home for the holiday.

Jake and I are sent to a small religious settlement not far from Jerusalem. After Survival Week, it's like being assigned to a vacation resort. We have a house trailer to ourselves, complete with our own shower and a kitchen in which to cook up our personal specialties: Jake turns out huge omelettes; I make a beef and sweet corn stew, an invention of my own. After weeks of eating *manot krav*, whatever we make tastes like gourmet cooking.

We luxuriate in being on our own. Except for guard duty and occasional radio contact with the company's second in command, we have no specific duties and no one to supervise us. And yet, when we have settled in, we find ourselves seated at a table cleaning our rifles.

The families in the settlement are religious Jews who feel they are fulfilling a pioneering mission by living on the West Bank. They are young families, with small children. Decent, friendly people who treat us as honored guests because we are there guarding their settlement and because we are Jews away from home on Rosh Hashanah. On each of the three days that we are there, someone from one family or another knocks at our door and invites us to the midday meal.

I get to know a couple named Cohen. Stanley Cohen is an immigrant from Brooklyn and his wife Elisheva is a sabra. They have very little in the way of worldly possessions, but they feel that they are leading dedicated lives. What strikes me is the contrast between the warmth with which they treat Jake and me, and the harshness with which they talk about their Arab neighbors, whom they regard as intruders on land that was given to the Jewish people by God.

They describe the history of the Jewish presence in this part of what they always call *Eretz Yisrael*, the Land of Israel. They talk of the Jews who have lived in Hebron for centuries.

"In 1907," says Elisheva, "there were a thousand Jews in Hebron. Twenty-two years later the Arabs rioted. They destroyed the Jewish quarter and massacred fifty-nine men, women, and children."

Stanley is quick to remind me that the Arabs drove the Old City's Jewish population from their homes during the War of Independence and then leveled the synagogues and desecrated the Jewish cemeteries.

"Look," he continues, "I've done my army service. I know what it means, from a military point of view, to have a border in which your enemies are only seventeen miles from the sea."

"Yes," says Elisheva, "that's one of the purposes we serve. We're a buffer, a military outpost. Because we're here, the Army doesn't have to assign additional manpower to the area."

"And," asks Stanley, "why shouldn't we live here? For centuries Jews were forbidden to own land. This should not be allowed to happen here, of all places."

After lunch, as the settlers continue Rosh Hashanah services in the trailer that has been turned into the synagogue, I walk along the perimeter of the village. Looking back, I see several trailers perched on tracts of bulldozed land. Then my eye moves down the hillside to "the path to the seven wells," which leads to the wadi floor. At the bottom, the land is a lush green, interspersed with small plots of date palms. My eye moves up to the terraces on which olive trees shimmer silver green, and to the tiny Arab village nestled into the curve of the hill a kilometer away.

I remember a comment that my Palestinian friend, Khalid, made as he explained that the bulldozer has become one of the symbols of the occupation. "How can a people who terrace the hillsides with a bulldozer preach love of the land to people who terrace it by hand?"

The village is close enough so that as the sun starts to set I hear the muezzin from the mosque calling the faithful to prayer. The long, mournful cry echos through the wadi, and resonates on the terraces on both sides of the valley.

As the call across the way subsides, I hear the *shofar* being sounded in the synagogue trailer in the settlement behind me. The last reverberations of the muezzin's call merge with the *tekiyah gedolah*, the long note on the ram's horn that signifies the end of Rosh Hashanah services.

The new year, 5747, has begun.

We're at the Western Wall. We are a third of the way through
our basic training and are about to be sworn into the Israeli
Army and into Nahal. Last night we did a ten-mile march to
earn the right to wear the Nahal shoulder tag. My company,
along with several others that began basic training at the
same time, are all milling about in the square. Relatives of
the soldiers are here; high-ranking officers are beginning to
show up. Flags of all sorts flutter in the evening breeze: the
Israeli flag, Nahal, Infantry, IDF banners. Half a dozen Hassidim, utterly oblivious to the mass of soldiers behind them,
are passionately at prayer beside the Wall. A small cluster of
women in the women's section are following their example.
The sun is going down after a hot day, and already, because
of Jerusalem's altitude, the air is turning brisk.

Just last week, a hand grenade was thrown into a crowd of
Givati infantrymen and their families celebrating a similar
ceremony. A soldier's father was killed and seventy people,
soldiers and civilians, were injured. Instinctively, I look
around to see if any extra security measures have been
taken, then I realize how ridiculous the thought is. What
better security can we have than the presence of several
hundred armed soldiers in the square?

But when I raise my eyes, I see that we are, in fact, being
guarded. There are patrols of soldiers on the surrounding
rooftops and on the staircases behind us, because now we
receive the order to hand our rifles over to our company
commanders. The point of the ceremony is that we will be
officially asked to receive a rifle in one hand and the Bible in
the other.

The order comes and we're lined up by companies facing
the Wall. The murmuring of the civilians subsides so that we
can hear the exhortations of the speakers standing on a temporary platform before us. Our base commander, Commander D., tells us that though our training will be hard, it

will be worth it. That it is an honor to serve our country. That Nahal is a proud unit with a distinguished history. Commander C., the head of the Infantry, is equally illuminating. What comes through to me is that these men are more used to action than to speech.

Finally, Commander D. moves front and center once again and shouts, "Thus you swear:

> I swear and pledge in all righteousness to be loyal to the State of Israel, to her laws and her government and to accept unconditionally and without reservation the discipline of the IDF, to follow all orders given by my commanders, and to dedicate all of my energy and even sacrifice my life in defense of the homeland and the liberty of Israel.

"Company Aleph, do you swear?"

Company Aleph shouts in unison, *"Ani nishba,* I swear."

I'm enjoying the theatricality of the event. Enjoying, too, standing comfortably here in Jerusalem instead of running around on some mountaintop picking the thorns out of my elbows the way I did last week. I enjoy the surge of energy taking place around me. And then, without warning, I feel uncomfortable. Something is missing.

Commander D. shouts, "Company Bet, do you swear?"

Again, I hear voices in unison: *"Ani nishba!"*

I know what's troubling me. It isn't that I'm here without any members of my family to cheer for me in the crowd. It's that, after so many weeks of basic training, I feel naked without my rifle.

Commander D. calls out, "Company Gimmel, do you swear?" By now it is dark. Torches cast shadows on the Wall.

Company Gimmel, which is made up mostly of Orthodox soldiers who will take no oath to anyone but God, respond in unison, *"Ani matzhir,* I promise!"

"Company Daled, do you swear?"

I'm in Company Daled. "I swear!"

The torches flicker as company after company repeats its oath. Finally we are turned over to our platoon commanders. Lieutenant Eli calls us forward. One by one we approach and salute. Then he hands each of us a rifle, which we take in one hand, and a Bible, which we receive with the other.

6
_____

Dear Grandma,
This will be quick because I don't really have much time. So much is happening to me and around me that I have trouble understanding it myself, much less trying to explain it to you. The Army is trying to get me in shape to function under battle conditions. That requires that I develop a whole new definition of my capabilities. On top of that, I'm also trying to keep my dignity and my sense of humor. It's not easy.

The training I'm getting is so intense it's sometimes hard to keep in mind just what it is a soldier is being trained to do.

The officers and noncoms are good. The guys I'm training with are great.

I hope all's well with you,
A.

P.S. Thanks for the scarf. Beautiful though it is, I probably won't get much chance to wear it this year. The Army seems to frown on plaid.

It has been raining sporadically for the last couple of weeks of basic training, but yesterday, the rainy season officially began. Now, we are being trucked to a base "somewhere in the center of the country." When we arrive, we set out our tents in the form of a U.

Soldiers, at the beginning of training, sometimes experience a condition called *helem bakum*, induction center shock. It can last several weeks while the trainee tries to trade his civilian reflexes for military ones; tries to adjust to sleepless nights, to people yelling at him. The trainee responds mechanically to orders. Every day that passes seems cut up into tiny segments and each segment is curiously surrounded by fog.

As a way of dissipating the fog, of relinking the segments of one's day, of adjusting to the Army, the trainee discovers that he forms friendships based on how well he can work with someone instead of on mutually shared interests.

The case of Tal is instructive.

In the meetings we all attended before we were inducted into the Army, Tal and I had formed a friendship. He is a South African with an easygoing manner and a well-developed taste (which I share) for jazz. I enjoyed talking with him whatever the subject—music, South Africa, Israeli politics.

Once we were in the Army together, his laid-back manner took on another meaning. He was, for example, invariably late. And being late was an offense that could get the whole platoon punished. If we had thirty seconds left to stand formation, there was Tal, slowly putting on his socks. If we had a minute and a half left, he managed to discover that he needed a shave. We got so used to his problems that we left a space in one of the back rows of the formation hoping that he could sneak into it without being caught. Otherwise, the whole platoon would be sent running for not falling in on time.

My own theory was that Tal was locked in some Einsteinian time warp in which he actually worked faster than all of us. So fast that the time frame in which he was enclosed was on a completely different scale from the one in which we lived. That, or something like that, had to be the case. How else could anybody be so consistently slow?

And yet, pressure from the instructors or the other guys never fazed him. One day as we were scurrying to get ready for the morning inspection, I heard him humming a mellow version of "Summertime" as he swept the walkways. The idea of "easy livin' " and "fish jumpin' " there on our training base was so ludicrous that it brought a smile to my lips as I hunted in the dirt for cigarette butts. So ludicrous that I joined in.

> Summertime and the livin' is easy.
> Fish are jumpin'
> And the cotton is high . . .

By the end of the first stanza, most of the other guys in the platoon had joined us in song. Guys were leaning on their brooms and rakes, each singing in his own language and in his own key:

> Your daddy's rich
> And your mamma's good-lookin'
> So hush little baby
> Don't you cry.

"I'll make you cry," came the voice of Sergeant Moshe from behind. The sentence was in Hebrew except for the English "cry," which Moshe pronounced with an Israeli guttural so harsh it sounded like a dog growling. "You have time to sing, you have time to run," he barked.

As we started our run around the bathroom, Tal and I

grinned at each other as if to say, "If you have to be punished for something, it might as well be for 'Summertime.'"

Now, as Nathan and I are setting up our tent, along comes Tal. As I watch him trudge up the path, I realize that, under the pressure of *helem bacum,* I've been focusing on getting my own work done as quickly as possible and distancing myself from Tal and guys like him. Guys I would like in the "real world," but whose relaxed attitudes can hold me back here.

As I understand the Army better, however, my own *helem bacum* begins to dissipate and I am able to let more and more of the civilian in me touch my life as a soldier. I now carry notepaper with me so I can write letters in my rare free time. Or I carry a paperback book. Any standard-size paperback of less than 280 pages can be waterproofed in plastic and will fit into the pants pocket of my uniform. Bouncing around on trucks or buses, I managed to get through Mark Helprin's *Refiner's Fire* and Toni Morrison's *Song of Solomon.* Between training exercises or while standing in line for food, I read Kurt Vonnegut's *Galápagos.* And Yoni Netanyahu's *Self-Portrait of a Hero.* From Yoni, the hero of the Entebbe operation, I get useful advice on how to treat blisters with a needle and thread, and the suggestion that a soldier should always carry writing paper or a book in his pocket.

Now here comes Tal, looking for a place to sleep. "I didn't get a tent assignment. I was off seeing the doctor."

So he says. I know that it's really because he's in that time warp of his. Just the same I realize that I like him. That I've missed him, and that it's dumb to distance myself from guys like him. Evidently Nathan is of my mind and we ask Tal to share our tent for the first night.

Besides, he's brought with him the most recent edition of the Jerusalem *Post.*

As Nathan and I set up the tent, Tal reads us the head-

line: "Mordecai Vanunu Jailed." Last September Vanunu
disappeared after selling his account of Israel's nuclear capabilities to the London *Sunday Times*. Nathan says, "Hey,
that's great. We're wasting our time here."

"Why?" I ask.

"The world now assumes that we have nukes. So infantry
is either redundant or irrelevant. We can pack up and go
home."

Tal reads, "The Iceland Summit: An Analysis."

"There it is again," says Nathan. "Now that the super-
powers have agreed to make war obsolete, we're redundant
or irrelevant. We can go home."

"Let's go," I say. I like this.

"Wait a minute," says Tal. He reads a third headline that
quotes Yitzhak Shamir, who has recently taken over the
coalition government from the Labor Party's Shimon Peres.
"Shamir Vows to Strengthen Hold on All of 'The Land of
Israel.' "

"So much for that," says Nathan. "Let's get the damn tent
up."

I pound in another stake.

A minute later, I look up and see clouds darkening the western sky. Already, I can see the path the rain will take, pour-
ing down the hillsides on either side of us. A swift mental
calculation tells me that any minute now the total surface
runoff of a four-square-mile area will be flowing through our
tent. I look longingly toward a reserve base some distance
above us, where smoke is rising from an indoor kitchen and
where there are empty twelve-man tents with concrete foun-
dations. Off to my left, I see Sergeant Moshe covering our
equipment and our supply of *manot krav* with vinyl in antici-
pation of the downpour.

I keep pounding stakes.

Putting up a tent with Nathan is always an experience. A

tall, muscular guy with dark wavy hair, he stands in the middle of the area that will be covered by our tent. He holds the tent poles straight while I scurry around driving in stakes and tightening ropes. If he contributes little to the tent-raising process, it's not because he's stupid. No. He's brilliant. Very brilliant. So brilliant he has a hard time doing anything as mundane as putting up a tent.

He grew up in Washington D.C., where at various times he was a long-distance runner who also played basketball and baseball. At Columbia, where he was working on an M.A. in comparative literature, he was offered a Woodrow Wilson Scholarship just as he discovered Zionism. He turned down the Woodrow, packed his bags, and moved to Israel.

In his *ulpan*, the language program he was sent to on a large kibbutz in the center of the country, he achieved near fluency in Hebrew in a matter of months. When our *garin* was being formed, Nathan chose to be sent to a border kibbutz where the apple orchards in which he worked run parallel to the Lebanese border. From his kibbutz at night he could see the lights of the Israeli border settlement Kiryat Shmona and the Hula Valley settlements to the east, and the Lebanese villages of Marhaba and Taibe to the west.

Once he was in the Army, Nathan progressed with great speed, advancing from Hebrew class four to class five, the highest level. Physically, he was equally powerful, able to sustain the longest marches, often carrying the loads of other guys without complaining.

But he was absolutely incapable of doing anything that required technical skill. He was consistently last when we had to take our Galil rifles apart and put them together again. He couldn't figure out how to put his gun strap on, and for months he wore a raggedly camouflaged helmet that was so small he could never get it to sit properly on his head. The only reason he has a sharp-looking helmet now is that when Alan, one of the other Americans, was sent off to a medic's course a few weeks ago, he gave Nathan his helmet and signed off on Nathan's.

When we were first sent to the firing range, each of us was issued six shells that we were supposed to fire on semi-automatic from a prone position. The idea was to get us acquainted with our weapons. In groups of four we were led onto the range by Sergeant Ronni, who turned us over to Lieutenant Eli. Eli had us lie down facing a green man-shaped target thirty yards away while he drummed firing range rules and wisdom into us: "Keep your barrel down range. Keep your safety on until you're ready to fire. Breathe normally. Release the safety to semi-automatic. Hold your breath on an exhale. Slowly, gently *squueeeeeeze* the trigger. Raise your right leg when you're done firing. OK. Now, each of you at your own target. Six shells, at your own pace. *Esh,* fire."

It's a simple-enough sequence, but Nathan couldn't do it. Perhaps in his brilliant mind he was calculating shell velocity, wind direction, and the relationship of relative humidity to the trajectory of the shells. Or what is more likely, he was confronting the fact that each round fired represented a human life possibly lost at his hands. Whatever the reason, he couldn't pull the trigger.

Lieutenant Eli, watching him, didn't know or care about Nathan's reasons for not firing. What he wanted was for every soldier in his platoon to be able to fire the damn rifle at need.

"All right," he shouted. "Everyone off the firing range. No, not you, Nathan. You stay here." Puzzled, we moved off the firing range and formed a little crowd nearby.

"Now, Nathan," said Lieutenant Eli, his voice level. "What you're holding in your hands is a Galil rifle. Right?"

"Right."

"And it's a weapon, right?"

"Yes, sir."

"Good. You understand that. Now, you lie down and face the target with your gun pointing at it. Is that clear?"

"Yes sir." Nathan lay down.

"Now, when I say *esh,* you fire, dammit. *Esh!*"

A pause. Then, *kpow.*

"Again, *esh!* Faster."

Kpow.

"Three shots. Faster. *Esh!*"

Kpow. Kpow. Kpow.

"Dammit, Nathan, there's a son of a bitch out there who's coming up the hill at you! *Esh!*"

Kpow.

"He wants to kill you! *Esh!*"

Kpow.

"And he will if you don't kill him first. *Esh!*"

Kpow.

"On automatic. *Esh!*"

Kpow pow.

"No, dammit. He's trying to kill you, man. Give him the whole damn clip on automatic. *Esh!*"

Kpow-pow-pow-pow-pow-pow-pow-pow-pow-pow-pow! Click.

"Good. He's dead and you're alive. That's it. Dismissed."

Later, as Nathan walked by me with his eyes on the ground, I went over thinking he needed consoling, but I had hardly cleared my throat when he looked up. He was wearing the widest grin I've ever seen on anyone and his eyes were twinkling. There was a slow curl of smoke still rising from the muzzle of his Galil.

I like talking with Nathan. He has a wide-ranging and imaginative mind and he seems to have read everything. It's something in basic training to have a buddy who wants to set me straight on what Dostoevsky really meant when he wrote *Crime and Punishment.* "No, no," Nathan insists, "it's a study in responsibility, not character. Sonya is the key, not Raskolnikov. Jesus is more relevant to the story than Freud." I don't know whether Nathan is right or not, but I sure like hearing what he has to say. It's refreshing to remember that there are issues larger than those posed by the Army. When he becomes my tentmate during basic training, I don't mind at all the relationship we establish. I set up the tent and he keeps me sane.

Having pitched our own tent, Nathan and I and a bunch of the other guys are ordered to put up a twelve-man tent for Lieutenant Ehud, the company commander.

At the beginning of our training, Lieutenant Ehud was our mystery man. We supposed he existed, but no one ever saw him. A civilian friend of Ehud's came to the base one day. Unable to find the command post, he asked me for help. As we walked along he said, "So, Ehud's your company commander, eh. He's pretty *gung ho,* isn't he?" He used the Hebrew word *mur'al,* which means, literally, "poisoned."

"Yes, s——" Talking to civilians, I forget that I don't have to say "sir."

"Well, how do you feel about him?"

How do I feel? It's like asking, "How do you feel about gravity?" It's there. It's undeniable.

In those early days, I knew he was there by his work, which was the overriding force behind everything that happened in our company. He organized our training schedules and designed the exercises himself. He planned our marches and led them. He was responsible for the company's food, ammunition, and supplies. Later, he would take us through our advanced infantry training and through Lebanon. In short, he had the responsibility for every detail of the lives of several dozen men for more than a year.

First Lieutenant Ehud is only twenty-three years old—one year older than Second Lieutenant Eli and three years younger than myself.

As our training progresses, he becomes more visible. I am startled by how much he looks like a commander: Five feet ten inches tall, barrel-chested, he stands ramrod straight. He carries a CAR-15 rifle, which is a shorter version of the M16 assault rifle. He carries it on an extra-long strap so that he can sling it casually over his shoulder, but I notice that his right hand is always on the grip of the gun and his index finger always hovers over the trigger. I'm told that he is an Ashkenazi Jew, but with his dark skin, black hair, and black eyes, he could easily be of Sephardic origin.

I got my first look at him two months into basic training when the word reached us that he was actually going to conduct our inspection himself. No one with a rank that high had ever inspected us before. For two days straight we prepared for his visit. We polished everything but the bullets in our ammunition belts and the place was spotless. Then, when it was all ready, we stood at attention beside our beds waiting for him to finish his inspection of the other platoons so he could come to us. We waited. And we waited.

That was when I discovered that people share with horses the ability to fall asleep standing up. It's a short sleep and fitful—you usually wake up before you hit the ground. But it can be done, and it is, sort of, restful. Later, I would learn to walk in my sleep, but that's still miles down the road.

After we had spent two and a half hours of dozing at attention, the mysterious Lieutenant Ehud suddenly appeared. And then I found out why he was late. His contact with each of us was anything but cursory. He called us by our first names, which surprised me because I had thought that we were as invisible to him as he was to us. As he spoke to us, one by one, he asked dozens of questions about equipment and combat preparedness. He wanted to know if we understood the principles behind the Galil automatic rifle's firing mechanism, and whether we knew the difference between that and what made the MAG machine-guns work.

What was the reason for requiring each man to fill his canteen to the top? And what happened if you accidentally fired an RPG (rocket-propelled grenade) into the ground in front of you? (The theoretical answer: nothing. But I wouldn't want to try it.)

Going from soldier to soldier, he discussed with us our understanding of our personal weapons, our squad weapons (mortars, RPG, MAG, and LAW), and even some weapons we had not yet encountered—lazer sights, night scopes. Then, with each of us, he turned from hardware to a few minutes of friendly conversation. He seemed to know all about us. He was familiar with Nathan's problems on the firing range and asked him how he felt about firing now. And he congratulated Alan, one of the guys from Chicago, whose sister had recently gotten married.

That, then, was Lieutenant Ehud, the young guy who shouldered the responsibility for our company. None of the men ever had a negative thing to say about him, though I once ran into an NCO on a bus who was willing to complain. "Man," he said, "have you any idea how hard he worked us? When you guys were snoring in your sleeping bags, Lieutenant Ehud kept us sergeants up till all hours of the night, grilling us to be sure we understood the plans for the next day. And the stuff he made us learn. Strange stuff . . ."

"Like what," I asked.

"Like he wanted us to understand the difference between the firing mechanism of the Galil automatic rifle and the MAG. Can you believe it?"

Now, working with the other guys to pitch the twelve-man tent for Lieutenant Ehud, some of us grumble, "We get the pup tents, they get the Hiltons. Whatever happened to the famous *dugma isheet*, leading by personal example the Army's always bragging about?"

Just then, one of two guys carrying a filing cabinet asks us to hold the tent flaps apart so they can bring it in, and as I look to the left, thirty paces away from the tent we have pitched, I see Lieutenant Ehud and Lieutenant Eli struggling to set up *their* pup tent in the wind. So much, then, for the Officers' Hilton.

Lieutenant Eli, our platoon commander, the same officer who finally got Nathan to fire his Galil, is a blue-eyed, tubby little guy. This far into basic, we're not even allowed to talk directly to him. If we have anything we want to tell him, we have to write a formal letter asking for an appointment. Just the same, aloof as he keeps himself, we get to know quite a bit about him.

Eli comes from one of the northern suburbs of Tel Aviv, a region of affluent homes. With all his urban sophistication, he is still a true idealogue, one of the shrinking number of Israelis who actually consider themselves Zionists. He has spent most of his Army service as a medic in a reconnaissance company. From there, he was selected for training as an infantry officer and did so well that, when he was commissioned, he was offered his choice of assignments: he could go back to a prestigious job in his recon company or he could take charge of a group of new immigrants and shape them up from basic training to border patrol. As a Zionist who wanted to do his part in the "ingathering of the exiles," he chose the immigrants.

Whether because of his politics or because of his innate decency, he makes us feel that he cares about us. I remember how he got David to overcome his bungling by letting him do his attack exercise in English, and the skillful way that he handled Nathan on the firing range. He conveys that sense of involvement with us in other ways as well.

A weekend in the Army usually begins with what's called a *Hamshishi,* which, loosely translated, means Thursfriday.

We'll start work early on Thursday morning, doing either a long exercise or a march, or sometimes both. Then we move right into a thorough inspection of whatever grounds we happen to be on at the time. In addition to cleaning up the grounds, we have to get our personal equipment battle-ready. We scrub our boots, our magazines, and our weapons. We clean our ammunition webbing, our sleeping bags, and our tents. We double-check our waterproofed personal bandages and our night-proofed dog tags. Finally, a little before sundown on Friday, we fall in for inspection. Then, except for those who have to do kitchen or guard duty, we are turned loose for the Sabbath.

At intervals of two or three weeks, when we have to stay on the base over the weekend, Lieutenant Eli makes a point of staying with us, even though, according to the officers' duty roster, he may be entitled to go home.

Lieutenant Eli does everything he can to make us understand why we are being asked to do the things we do. No matter what the scale of the exercise, he makes sure that each of us knows his task and how that task is related to what everyone else is doing. In an exercise involving a squad or a platoon, for instance, a machine gunner in an open field exercise will be told not only where to lay cover fire, but why that fire is important support to a force flanking around from the right. In a large-scale exercise, Lieutenant Eli makes sure that even a guy whose job is only to carry a jerry can is told exactly what the company or brigade plans are.

As part of our training, we spend a certain amount of time listening to analyses of important battles that the Israel Defense Force has fought. We study the techniques of trench warfare that Company Bet used in the battle for the Golan Heights in 1967. Or we analyze the tank battles that were fought when those same Heights were defended in 1973. And we discuss Company Aleph's inability to hold a fortified position in the Sinai Desert in 1973. When Lieutenant Eli plays us the tape of the final radio transmission in which the commander of Company Aleph announces his decision to surrender to the Egyptians, I get impatient and raise my hand.

"Yes?" says the lieutenant.

"I don't get it. Why are we spending so much time studying Israeli battle failures? How is this supposed to improve our morale?"

Lieutenant Eli's reply is short. "Morale can't be based on illusions. We're not *Supermanim.* Those lost battles are where the lessons lie."

Lieutenant Eli is a fine officer, but he's far from perfect. When he makes mistakes, they aren't trivial, and we feel them at once.

Sometimes he reads the guys wrong, particularly the immigrants, some of whom he has punished for being *fucky-onairim* when it was actually that the soldier couldn't express himself adequately in Hebrew. Johnnie, from Los Angeles, tried hard to be a good soldier, but precisely because he was trying so hard, he managed to put the wrong emphasis on his words so that he sounded sarcastic. Once, during an inspection, Lieutenant Eli showed Johnnie where he had left a dirty spot on the 52-millimeter mortar. Johnnie, who was trying to say, "Thank you for showing me, sir," managed, because of his San Fernando Valley accent and shaky Hebrew, to say, "What makes you think you could do better?" Lieutenant Eli was not amused and poor Johnnie had his Shabbat pass lifted.

But Lieutenant Eli made his biggest mistake because he is a man of deep conviction. When we immigrants finished our *ulpan,* the powers that be decided to send one third of our group to another platoon and replace those guys with a sabra *garin.* The idea, I suppose, was to create a melting pot.

But there was trouble immediately. The differences in age, education, and motivation of the two groups were too great to be reconciled, especially under the stress of training. As we were to find out later, sabras and immigrants can and do get on very well, but not until later on. Here, at the beginning, the mechanical mixing of the two groups produced a "popcorn situation." With a little heat and pressure, it exploded. There was constant squabbling, and on a hot afternoon, a fist fight between David, one of the American machine gunners, and Gavriel, a soldier from the development town of Yavne, over a knocked over tent pole.

Lieutenant Eli was, at first, against the idea of the melting pot, but when he saw that his superiors were committed to the experiment, he decided to make our platoon a shining example of the absorption process. Later, when Eli's superiors were willing to retreat from their position, Lieutenant Eli dug his heels in. He was determined to show that he could make us all get along—for the greater good of Israeli society and for the Jewish people as a whole.

But we wouldn't, and we didn't. Our differences grew and multiplied. We accused the sabras of being babies, and they were; they accused us of being square, which we certainly were. Finally, Lieutenant Eli succumbed to reality. He re-requested a reorganization of the platoon. The sabras went back to Company Bet and our immigrants came back home to us.

At first, the sound of the rain is only a gentle pitta-pat on the company headquarters tent we have just pitched. Then the downpour sounds like a continuous drumroll, until finally we seem to be in a tent pitched just under Niagara Falls. The earth around us turns instantly into a marsh then, moments later, into a lake. The sky is leaden and I can see that the rain will be around for a while. We scurry off to our pup tents to salvage our duffel bags containing our fresh uniforms and underwear. Then we scoot back to take refuge in the headquarters tent, leaving our sleeping bags and personal equipment behind to survive the storm as best they can.

Normally, the Army would have us out training in a storm like this, as we will later today and all the rest of the week. But for the moment our sergeants leave us alone in our refuge as they make themselves comfortable in the supply tent.

From a group of wet soldiers crouching in a tent we turn without much trouble into a bunch of guys having a party. Brian, one of our Englishmen, turns up the small radio he always carries and we hear the voice of Shlomo Artzi singing *Nirkod Nishkach*, "We'll Dance and Forget":

> *Alone, you dance, confident of your steps.*
> *Suddenly you trip and I come for you.*
> *I'm not frustrated when the band stops playing.*
> *They close here at five, so we still have a*
>   *minute.*
>
> *And you whisper:*
> *"Let's dance and we'll forget.*
> *We'll dance together,*
> *We'll dance and forget . . ."*

Some guys are sent to the supply tent to bring back benches. One by one, we dig into our kitbags and come up with our stash of *chuparim*—the cookies, candies, and potato chips with which we supplement our field ration diet. Entire week's supplies are sacrificed for the greater good of our impromptu *erev garinim*.

The Nahal branch of the Army does its best to keep up the morale of its *garinim*. All members of a *garin*, combat and noncombat groups, are trained on parallel schedules so that major events, like the end of a phase of training, can be celebrated together. Occasionally, as at the end of a beret march or on certain afternoons when we are not required to be in the field, the whole *garin* will be brought together for a couple of hours, just to drink coffee, eat potato chips, and shmooze. Such a social event is called an *erev garinim.*

So, though we're without our girlfriends and our noncombat friends, and the mud is starting to ooze into the tent, we're making the most of what we've got. Tommy, from Manchester, has a combat specialty we all appreciate. No matter where we are, no matter how arduous our situation, he always manages to provide us with something hot to drink, and he doesn't fail us now. He comes in out of the rain, smiling broadly, carrying containers of steaming Turkish coffee that he liberated from the battalion kitchen.

We drink, we relax, we talk about our officers and sergeants. We talk about the weather and hope that the storm will keep up. "Even if it doesn't," points out my friend Jake, "we'll still spend the week indoors." He's right. This week we're learning house-to-house combat.

All of our training is based on a pattern we learned several weeks ago when we were being trained to fight in three-man teams. First, you lay cover fire and then attack from the side. Everything else is commentary. Once we understand and perfect that strategy, the only variables will be in size and combat environment. When we were fighting as a three-man unit, one man was responsible for the cover fire while the other two attacked from the side. In larger actions, a squad, a platoon, or a company may lay cover fire while a proportionately sized group of men attacks from the side. So a squad may have a MAG, a 52-millimeter mortar, and a sniper, while a company may employ .50 caliber machine guns, 60-millimeter mortars, and a "Maklar" 40-millimeter grenade thrower. The side attacks may come from infantrymen on foot, in armored personnel carriers, or in sophisticated actions, from helicopters.

In military lingo, the places where we may need to fight are called "combat environments." They can include open fields, orchards, trenches, city streets, and in the basaltic Golan Heights, volcanic cones, which make excellent strategic points and are a bitch to train on.

When we move on to advanced training, everything we do will be based on the same diagram of action, but the scale will be much larger. We'll work up to a full mobilization of the Northern Command, where the preparatory work will be done by Intelligence and Reconnaissance units, the Air Force, and Combat Engineers. Cover fire will include artillery, tank, and anti-aircraft units, while the side attacks will be a combination of Navy, tanks, and helicopter-borne or mechanized infantry. The gathering up of the mock dead and wounded is handled by the medics and doctors of the Medical Corps, in keeping with one of the IDF's most fundamental tenets: "Never, never leave any dead or wounded behind on the field of battle."

Last week, we were introduced to "NBC" warfare. N stands for nuclear. Our instructors quip, "If that happens, there's nothing you can do about it. So not to worry." B stands for biological, and again, there's nothing to be done. C, which stands for chemical warfare, is taken more seriously, especially since the Iraqis have shown no hesitation about introducing chemical weapons into the Middle East, and because it is known that Syria has been expanding its chemical warfare arsenal. Wherever our company goes, we carry an emergency case of gas masks, protective blankets, and neutralizing powder. What C training mostly involves is learning to run and maneuver while wearing a gas mask. We also modify our regular short exercises. In addition to doing them "wet" and "dry," with and without firing live ammunition, we do them also while wearing gas masks.

To be effective in combat, each infantryman is assigned a dual, even a triple, combat role. First and foremost we are riflemen who have achieved "expert level" scores of three and five during basic training and later, seven, during the squad leader's course. Normally, we carry our rifle, which weighs about eleven pounds loaded, eight other full magazines—thirteen pounds—and two full water bottles with a combined weight of four and a half pounds. That then, is an infantryman's normal load, which comes to about thirty pounds if we include the weight of the ammunition webbing.

On top of all that, midway through basic training we are assigned *pakalim,* the squad loads or weapons for which, depending on our strength and skills, we are responsible.

A big guy who is also fast and dependable is issued the FN MAG 7.62-millimeter machine gun. The MAG is a heavy gun, but because of its long-range accuracy and its capacity for relentless and damaging firepower, it has been the main IDF infantry support weapon for more than twenty-five years. A MAGist has to be willing to work hard, first, because the gun is hard to keep clean, and then, because its own weight plus that of several hundred rounds of ammunition will load a soldier down by an additional twenty-five to thirty pounds. The MAGist has to be both nimble and dependable because he is either providing cover fire, in the course of which he is likely to have his unit in his sights, or he is on one of the flanks beside the commanding officer covering the front line. Because of the hard work and responsibility, the MAG is a prestigious *pakal* and a good MAGist will sometimes be sent home for an extra weekend in recognition of the importance of his job. My friends, Jake, David, who had such problems with the Hebrew relay orders, and Bill, a burly, red-headed ex-football player from Baltimore—all of them Americans—are each issued a MAG.

On one exercise, Jake, who is from New York, loads himself up with equipment. The MAG rests on his shoulders. Belts of ammunition hang from his webbing. Two fragmentation grenades are clipped to his shoulder strap. Looking down at his deadly load, he shakes his head.

"What is it?" I ask.

"With all of this, I still wouldn't get on the A Train."

A soldier who is better at taking on responsibilities than at carrying loads may be assigned to carry *rarnats,* rifle-fired grenades. A "rarnatist" has one of the lightest squad loads to carry. A full pack of fifteen grenades weighs only about fifteen pounds. The grenades look like very high-tech arrows whose heads explode on impact and they are carried in a quiver on the rarnatist's back. The grenades are fitted onto the rifle barrel, from which they are propelled by the explosion of a blank shell. The rarnatist, too, has to be a man of good judgment, because like the MAGist, he has to fire his grenade ahead of the charging line in an attack. Once when Brian was covering for Matti, our permanent rarnatist, he fired a little low during a charge and came close to taking out several senior officers who were on the sidelines observing. They grimaced at his ineptitude.

Most officers and some of the NCOs have radiomen walking behind them. The standard field radio is an AN/PRC-77. A stripped "sport" radio weighs less than twenty pounds, but by the time a gung-ho officer has loaded it up with flare gun, helicopter landing signal kit, smoke grenades, signal flags, a signal mirror, and a mine prod, it can weigh better than thirty pounds. A new Israeli-made 91 model, which is several pounds lighter and more versatile, is being introduced.

There are certain advantages to being a radioman. He gets to hear all the communications on his handset so he's one of the few people in a unit who actually knows what's going on in an exercise or action. And the unit relies on him for information and gossip.

On the other hand, there are disadvantages. We are told

that in trench warfare a company commander's life expectancy is about eight seconds from the time he enters an enemy trench. If the radio operator who accompanies him is lucky, he may live as long as twelve seconds.

I'm issued a field radio.

Other *pakalim* include the 52-millimeter mortar, the heaviest *pakal* of all, which, with its accompanying bombs, weighs forty pounds. Then there are ten-liter jerry cans for water, which weigh twenty-two pounds full. There are the RPGs, which, with their grenades, weigh twenty pounds; the LAW, light antitank weapon, which weighs fifteen pounds; and the M203 grenade launcher, which is usually attached to an M16 assault rifle. The rifle, together with its grenades, weighs about twelve pounds. Finally there are the stretchers which, when no one is being carried on them, weigh twelve pounds.

A couple of guys in every unit are called "empty backs." What they get to carry depends on the exercise or action in which we are involved. Sometimes they carry additional bullets, grenades, mortars, collapsible ladders, stakes, ropes, mines. Or else they help the overloaded guys when they can.

The strangest *pakal* each of us carries is a small waterproofed kit called a *pakal haballa,* which consists of a shoelace, several matches, and a razor blade. This curious collection no longer seems so curious after I've taken the demolitions course. The shoelace is used to tie an explosive charge where you want it; the blade is used to cut the fuse to the right length and angle. As for the matches? Well, the matches . . .

Aside from being trained in the use of our rifles and our *pakalim,* we are also sent to all kinds of courses to learn a *miktzoah,* a "profession." The longest and most intense of these courses is the three-month combat medic's course. Our unit sends Peter, Alan, and Danno to the course. Alan and

Peter pass it, but Danno comes back to us and is designated as an empty back.

The best marksmen in the platoon take a five-week sniper's course. The standard sniper's weapon is a 7.62-millimeter M21, a more accurate version of the M14. Some units use a sniper's version of the Galil, and a night sniper may use an M16 fitted with a starlight night-scope. Commando units often use sophisticated laser and infrared sighting equipment.

A sniper has an enviable position in a platoon—of all of us, he has the least weight to carry. Because he has to be kept maneuverable, his *pakal* consists only of his rifle, extra magazines, and a set of binoculars. Our platoon's sniper is André, a tall, whimsical Parisian.

Some of us attend courses that teach us how to drive APCs, armored personnel carriers, or courses that develop our proficiency with company weapons: 60-millimeter mortars, .50 caliber machine guns, and the Maklar, an automatic weapon which fires a series of grenades over a distance of a couple of kilometers the way a machine gun fires bullets.

In addition to the specialized instruction, we are expected to attend refresher courses on our own *pakalim*. And of course we are held responsible for a working knowledge of all the squad weapons. The point our instructors make is that our versatility is the one advantage we have over the enemy.

Versatility! By the end of basic training, I will be a rifleman, expert level five; a licensed APC driver; a proficient operator of both the 77 and 91 model field radios; and a fully trained Maklar 40-millimeter grenade thrower. By the end of my Army service I will have upped my rifleman expert level to seven; I will have added a three-week paratroop course and a three-month squad commander's course to the list.

I wonder how I'll fit all that on a résumé.

The base camp where our tents are pitched is now, after that happy rainstorm, situated in the very middle of Israel's newest lake. It is a couple of miles from a village which was built to be destroyed. It is the site for our house-to-house combat training. The houses have no electricity, plumbing, or floors, and the walls are covered with thick tar paper to cut down on ricochets and flying debris. What they do have is a maze of winding staircases and rooms within rooms that are intended to simulate the trickiest situations we may run into. Every morning, like suburban commuters, we make our way to the village where we spend the day "taking" a room, a house, or a street. In the evening, we march back home. At the end of the week, our company will have to take the entire village—four times: first dry, then wet, by day; then dry, then wet, by night. Wet, of course, means firing live ammunition; dry means going "bang, bang."

The house-to-house combat training makes us confront a couple of things about what we're doing. With everything we've done up till now—military theory classes, practice on the firing range, and open field warfare exercises—it has been easy to forget or overlook just what it is we're being trained to do. We have been shooting at balloons or targets. Even the human-shaped targets we shoot at represent real people about as much as the little figures in a Wolf Patrol video game.

But being trained to do house-to-house fighting is different. One can't dissociate walking through a doorway from people. Doorways have specifically human meanings. People live on the other sides of doorways. Real people. Your friends. The people in your own home.

In my first solo wet exercise, I take a room just as I have been taught to while Lieutenant Eli looks on. I come up to the side of the doorway, crouch, and pull off two rounds

while I check what's inside. I pull the pin on a hand grenade, release the firing mechanism, and hold it for a second
so that if someone is inside he won't have time to throw it
back out at me. Then I toss the grenade and wait for its thud
on the other side of the wall. When it comes, I go in, firing
systematically around the room. Usually, it takes most of a
magazine to take one room. When I yell out that the room is
"pure," I go outside while Lieutenant Eli comes in to check
the silouhette targets that were my enemies in the room.

"Nice shooting," he says as he tosses me the head of one
of the targets. It's been shot clean off at the neck.

There is another thing that strikes me about house-to-house
combat: here, more than in any other kind of training, our
lives will depend on how closely we work together. Usually,
three people are needed to "take" an enemy room. Two guys
go in together with rifles firing at cross angles just inches in
front of each other while a third man covers the doorway.
Often, other soldiers will be firing in the next room or building or across the street. And though from very early in our
training we've been told that "the Army is not an insurance
company," combat training can get a little hairy if you're
teamed up, for instance, with a guy like Mario.

Mario may be the funniest guy in the platoon. He is a
small, balding Italian from Milan whose English is taken
almost entirely from Bruce Springsteen songs. He's a good-
natured guy who hasn't got a mean or cowardly bone in his
body. But during exercises, as soon as the shooting starts,
Mario shuts down. He doesn't yell or panic. He just becomes
completely disoriented.

In open field warfare, if a soldier runs in the wrong direction—even if he shoots in the wrong direction—there is
plenty of room to absorb his mistake. It's even harder for
him to go wrong in trench warfare because all he has to do is
follow the lines of the trench. But a couple of soldiers enter-

ing an enemy room move according to a very detailed chore-
ography and each man has to know his place and his steps.
Which explains why I'm very nervous about being teamed
up with Mario for house-to-house fighting. In our very first
"dry" exercise, Mario entered the room first and went immediately into the wrong corner. As I followed him, I found
myself looking down the barrel of his gun.

Luckily, no one was hurt either then or later. In fact, our
platoon has had very few training accidents—shin splints,
twisted ankles, a dislocated shoulder, and a broken leg. This
is surprising when you consider how much lead flies around
in the course of training, and the fact that both Lieutenant
Ehud and Lieutenant Eli routinely shoot in the direction of
trainees—either to simulate battle conditions or simply to
emphasize how angry they are at something the trainee has
done wrong.

We did have one weapons-related accident when Yoni, one
of the sabras, fired an RPG whose exhaust vent was clogged
with mud. Any rocket-fired weapon has to have a clean exhaust vent to allow the powerful back blast of the gun to
escape. Maybe Sylvester Stallone doesn't have to worry
about such details—in *Rambo II* Stallone is shown firing an
RPG at a Russian helicopter while his POW friends behind
him look on—but in the real world, that RPG's back blast
would have fried his friends to a crisp.

Things weren't that bad for Yoni. His RPG kicked, his
grenade fired wildly. The gunsight split Yoni's forehead and
the grenade exploded in the air. But after stitches and a
couple of days at home recuperating, Yoni is back with the
rest of us.

Other platoons haven't had our luck. I hear stories of
injuries and deaths in the course of large exercises or because of accidental firings. One lieutenant shows me the binoculars he had in his backpack when a nearby MAGist fired

accidentally in his direction. The binoculars still have the bullet embedded in the metal.

We're still in the twelve-man tent having our *erev garinim*. Tal, who, it turns out, really has been to see the doctor, brings us news of the cluster of sabras with whom, until a few weeks ago, we trained. They have been assigned to Company Bet, and things have not gone well with them—as we might have predicted. We had had problems of our own with them, first because of their youth, and then because their *garin* was simply not cut out to be in a combat unit. The official name of their *garin* is Garin Halom, "Dream Garin." But we had taken to calling it Garin Siyut, "Nightmare Garin."

Tal says, "Of the twelve guys we trained with, eight have had their profiles lowered." The eight guys Tal is talking about are now being trained to become noncombat soldiers: cooks, drivers, and supply clerks. "Of the other four guys, two are still combat soldiers, and the third is in the hospital after trying to commit suicide. Finally, there's Gavriel. Good old Gavriel."

David, who had the fist fight with Gavriel, looks up. "What happened to him?"

"He's in jail," says Tal. And that makes us all look up. "In jail?"

Nobody is quite surprised to learn that Gavriel is in jail.

The Army relies on several kinds of pressure to help it mold a guy into a soldier. First of all, there's the history of Israel. There is hardly an Israeli, sabra or immigrant, who doesn't know what role the Army has played in Israel's survival. An effective image, familiar to many, is a map of what the Middle East would look like had the Arab armies won in 1948, 1967, or 1973. It shows Syria extending south through the Galilee, Jordan west to the Mediterranean coast, and Egypt reaching north to Tel Aviv. Even those who question some of the Army's policies would never claim that the Army itself is unnecessary. The writer Amos Oz, one of the founders of Peace Now, for example, says emphatically, "I am a peacenik, not a pacifist."

The Army is interwoven into Israeli society—every citizen is required to do military service and every man continues to serve annually in the reserves until he reaches the age of fifty-five. And how well one has done in the Army can make a difference in the soldier's civilian life and career. Job applicants are asked about their service; a good record in the Army can enhance a résumé. Even driver's license applications have spaces for one's military ID and profile number. Families, of course, watch the progress of their sons and daughters in the Army closely and like to brag about their achievements.

Some units are perceived as top of the line. Pilots, commandos, and certain intelligence and infantry units take only volunteers. Spaces in these units are always filled.

Peer pressure also works to keep a soldier in line. And the pressure isn't only psychological. Since punishments are frequently meted out collectively, a soldier who regularly gets his unit into trouble can bring the wrath of his fellows down on him. There is, for instance, the punishment known as the "blanket party," during which the offending soldier has a blanket thrown over his head and is thoroughly pummeled by his buddies. Usually, the guy gets the message.

Usually, but not always. Not Gavriel. Gavriel was indifferent to the lessons of history, to the expectations of society, to the attitudes of the men in his unit. From the first moment of his Army service, it was clear that he did not fit, and was not going to be made to fit the Army's mold.

Gavriel didn't give a damn. A large, muscular North African with a left eye that tended to cross, he came into the Army from the development town of Yavne. He was present, however, in body only. Where his spirit was, I don't know. He smirked at the Army chain of command, was amused by the orders he was given, and laughed at the NCOs. None of the measures taken to discipline him had any effect. If we were made to run because he had been late, he would sit behind the bathroom building and encourage us as we ran. When he refused to get out of bed and was called out for individual punishment, he accepted stoically whatever was done to him. While we sat under a eucalyptus tree learning radio code, Gavriel was made to crawl belly down on a dirt track a few feet away. When he swore pleasantly at Sergeant Ronni, who was supervising his punishment, Ronni loaded Gavriel down with a twenty-two-pound jerry can to mark his displeasure. Gavriel accepted the additional weight and continued crawling back and forth along the track. When he passed us sitting comfortably in the shade, he paused long enough to wink.

When Gavriel really didn't want to be there, he just walked away. One night, on the return leg of a twelve-mile night march, we had to walk along a sand road in an orange grove with a three-foot drainage ditch running alongside it. The loose sand made for hard walking, but the night air was cool and perfumed with the fragrance of the orange blossoms. It was our third march that week and I was walking about two thirds of the way back in the column, thinking how tired I was of marches in general and of this one in particular. Gavriel, beside me, seemed to have been thinking similar thoughts. At a curve in the road I caught the gleam of Gavriel's undisciplined eye looking up at me from the ditch into which he had crawled.

"Get up out of there," I whispered. "Sergeant Moshe's right behind us. If I can see you, he can see you." But Gavriel lay still. We marched on and, sure enough, a minute later, the command came, "Platoon, halt." We stopped and I heard scuffling sounds and muffled shouts to the rear—muffled because night discipline prevents anyone, even an angry sergeant, from shouting aloud. Then there was Sergeant Moshe manhandling Gavriel as he pushed him in the direction of Lieutenant Eli at the front of the column. On Gavriel's face as he passed us was his usual somewhat absent smile.

Then we were moving again, with Lieutenant Eli setting the pace. Nathan, one of our strongest marchers, walked immediately behind him, and behind Nathan, marching briskly and in time with him, the still smiling Gavriel. It took me a moment to realize why: Gavriel's hands were tied and the rope binding them was attached to the striding Nathan's belt. Gavriel maintained the pace.

Gavriel's punishment, when we got back to the base, was confinement to his tent. It's a punishment that pleased him just fine.

Gavriel was a living reminder that, finally, the Army could not hurt you if you chose not to let it. What if you don't want to get out of bed? What if you don't want to do any of the things they want you to do? Well, they can make you run, stand you out in the sun, put a pack on your back, and make you crawl. They can take your Saturdays away. But if none of this bothers you and the idea of jail doesn't daunt you, then you've really limited their power over you. And the knowledge of that may be why, though we have sometimes paid for his rebellion, we have a sneaking admiration for Gavriel, who, Tal tells us, is now in jail for taking the base commander's Jeep for a joy ride.

Despite the drumbeat of rain on the tent roof, I look out through the tent flaps. I announce, unnecessarily, "It's still raining."

The next time I look out, I see Sergeant Moshe dashing down on the path from the reserve base. He stops at our tent to tell us angrily that we have twenty minutes to get ready to move. "Get your gear together," he roars, "then get over to the reserve base and divide yourselves up into the twelve-man tents. Get moving."

We don't wait for more encouragement. We pack up our soggy loads without even feeling their weight, and ignoring the mud and rain, we practically run up the hill to the twelve-man tents. But even as I run, I worry about our sleeping bags. Each of them has absorbed enough water to fill a small bathtub. Though by now I know that we can sleep in wet bags, I'm still very partial to dry ones.

But again, our grumpy Sergeant Moshe has anticipated our needs and has *do'egg*-ed, taken care of us. When we get to the reserve base, there he is standing beside a truck he must have called for earlier. A truck containing nothing but dry uniforms, blankets, and naturally, sleeping bags.

Sergeant Moshe has a knack for finding us good things. Our platoon seems to have newer magazines, more ammunition, and better load-bearing packs than other platoons. By the end of basic training, Moshe is taking certain trusted soldiers with him on "search and acquire" missions for our company. These guys patrol the base for any unattached equipment that might be useful to our company: ammunition, targets, tent stakes.

Sergeant Moshe's coup was acquiring the company's signboard.

We were assigned to patrol a national reunion of everyone who had ever served in the Nahal. The organizers of the reunion ordered a five-foot-high wooden sign to be built displaying the Nahal insignia: a scythe and a sword framed by two wreaths of olive leaves. No sooner did Sergeant Moshe see this sign than he vowed to have it for our company. Nobody, he reasoned, would need it after the reunion was over. Certainly nobody saw him and Jake, one of his trusted accomplices, sneaking the huge wooden placard past several hundred armed guards and several thousand ex-soldiers. The sign has been in the platoon's possession ever since.

In all my time in the Army, I rarely ate enough food and it was rarer still to find food that was any good. But Sergeant Moshe, with the help of guys who couldn't go out into the field because of sickness or injury, always whipped up a surprise to cheer the rest of us when we came back from some difficult exercise: potato pancakes or French toast, sweet fruit juice or Turkish coffee. At the end of a particularly long march, Moshe prepared Nescafé with milk, which, to an exhausted Israeli soldier, was true ambrosia.

In the tents, we divide ourselves as always into groups according to national origin. The American and the South African tents opposite each other on either side of the path; the European and South American tents alongside them.

In my tent, we organize our gear and get ready for a brief inspection. Though it is only 7 P.M., the guard list is already being read. It is the last official thing we do before we turn in for the night. Because of the storm and our move to this auxilliary base, we have had no training at all today.

I arrange my equipment next to my bed so I can find it easily in the dark when I get up to stand guard at 2:30 A.M. Shmuel, an accountant from South Africa, was responsible for the guard list this week and I'm satisfied that he's been doing it fairly. But not everyone else is and he's surrounded by guys complaining about their assignments. All I want is to sleep. I strip off my wet uniform, crawl into my sleeping bag, and yield to its warmth. Bill, the burly ex-football player from Baltimore, whose bunk is at the foot of mine, says, as he does every night, "Ah, this is the only part of the Army I like." I know just how he feels.

Jake, the guy in the bunk at my right, is also settling down. A tall, muscular guy from Scarsdale, New York, Jake has been picked to carry a MAG, and he literally flies through exercises with it, running faster with his heavy gun than guys with empty backs.

Yet he and the Army do not make a good fit, mostly because Jake hates discomfort. And the Army perpetually creates discomfort—which Jake tries to overcome. His complaint about his weak ankles has kept him out of several of our marches and he has been excused from some of our exercises because of his bad knees. Ever since mid-October, when the nights began to get a little nippy, Jake has been secretly carrying a compressible down sleeping bag, whose blue hood I now see peeking out of his ratty green army issue bag.

Tommy the Mancunian is sleeping next to Jake. Tommy is proud of his roots. He constantly reminds us that, "We build 'em *tuf* in Manchester." Despite that, and because he once spent two weeks in New York and Connecticut, he has decided that his true place is here with us in the American tent. He loves to talk about California women, New York pizzas, and what he calls, "Reese's Peanut Butter Cupcakes." What we like best about him is his irreverence.

One day, for example, when a high-ranking muckamuck lectured us about proper soldierly behavior, he ended by saying, "Remember, it's important for our image. Any of you who misbehave will find yourselves listed in my Black Book."

Tommy jumped up. Throwing his arms in the air as if begging for mercy, he squealed in falsetto horror, "Oh, no, sir. Please. Not the *Black Book!*" The officer joined in the explosion of laughter that followed.

Tommy's other big talent is his ability to find something hot for us to drink under any conditions, as he did this afternoon. He simply steals a pitcher of coffee or tea from a base kitchen. Or he sneaks into the kitchen past the wary and unforgiving cooks and makes the coffee or tea himself. Even in the field Tommy comes through, concocting a "solar tea" for us by scraping clean a field ration can, filling it with canteen water and tea bags, and letting the mixture stand out in the sun. The brew we get does, in fact, taste faintly like tea and goes down well after a meal.

Across from Tommy sleeps Alan, a thick-set guy from Chicago who keeps his hair cut short. Alan is very *mur'al*, gung ho. He also has a photographic memory, which makes him one of our unit's quickest learners. He's the first to know the parts of a gun, the week's vocabulary list, or the radio codes. He's so good at cleaning his Galil that Lieutenant Eli asks him to give us a demonstration on how to do it right. He also knows the words to all the pop songs, English or Hebrew, written in his lifetime. But Alan's real skill is falling in love.

A soldier in basic training has a hard time maintaining a love affair. A guy who has a girlfriend when he enters the Army is likely to lose her before his basic training is over. When he gets home for a rare weekend, he is so tired that he stumbles into his room late Friday afternoon. Barely remembering to lock up his gun, he collapses onto his bed and sleeps straight through until Saturday night, when he may wake briefly for dinner only to fall back asleep until he has to start getting ready to return to the base early Sunday morning. Love can triumph over such an impediment, but it has a hard time. So broken romances are a not unusual story.

But Alan, on his weekends, finds the time and energy to fall in love not once, but three times. Once on Friday afternoon on the bus going into town, once on Saturday morning when he is smitten by a *kibbutznikit*. Then, on Saturday night he is hopelessly entranced by a kibbutz volunteer he meets at a dance. His report of his experience is always the same: "It's for real. I've found her. She's the ideal woman. She's amazing. This time it's right."

Six times, eight times a month.

The core of the South African tent is a group of four who came to Israel together and now live on a new kibbutz in the Galilee. They are very tight and complement each other as soldiers. Shmuel, who was trained as an accountant has a linear, orderly mind. He is so systematic he is often asked to do the platoon's bookkeeping chores. He prepares guard lists, announces equipment changes, and records the week-end pass list.

Matti and Chris are the den mothers of the platoon. They are always available when anyone needs good advice or a confidant. Matti comes back from weekends excited by a new pie recipe or a knitting stitch he has learned. Chris glows when he talks about his girlfriend Marta, a blond sabra modern dancer. Chris and Matti are also dead shots with their squad weapons: Matti with the *rarnat* and Chris on the RPG.

Brian, the fourth member, has let his light curly hair grow to the maximum length the Army will allow. He's actually British, but because he belongs to the same youth movement as the other three guys, he makes his home on their kibbutz. He's an important part of the platoon both for his ability to carry heavy loads and, more importantly, because he always carries a pocket radio with him. As our days away from population centers pass, his radio news and entertainment become our sole link with the world outside. The radio is forbidden, lest he should listen to it while on guard duty, but Brian has been caught with it at inspection so many times (and he takes such good care of it) that Lieutenant Eli has succumbed and now inspects it for cleanliness along with Brian's rifle and magazines.

The truth is that Brian not only listens to the radio when he is standing guard, but then passes it along to the other guys on the night duty roster. A lonely hour in the middle of the night goes by a lot easier when it is enlivened by Army

Radio's "Don't Want to Sleep" soft rock show, or the Voice
of America's 2 A.M. news broadcast.

Most of the time, Brian is in a fantasy world that, from the
brief glimpses I've had of it, is several times more complex
and interesting than the world of only three dimensions in
which the rest of us are stuck. I've visited his room on the
kibbutz—you can't even see the walls. One is hidden by
stacks of games: "Dungeons and Dragons," "Stellar-Con-
quest," "Wizard Quest," "Storm-Bringer," and other fantasy and role-acting games.

Another wall is hidden by hundreds of science fiction and
fantasy books: *Lord of the Rings, The Worm Ourobouros,* and
the entire *Dune* series. The wall next to that one is the comic
book wall, whose shelves are crammed with boxes, cartons,
and drawers full of comic book titles from the last ten years:
Batman, Superman, Spider-Man, and *The Justice League of
America.* The last wall is covered by shelves containing hundreds of plastic, plaster, and pewter wizards, warriors, mi-
notaurs, dinosaurs, satyrs, and knights.

"Can you tell what order they're in?" Brian asks slyly.

I look for an organizing principle: color, size, chronology,
but I can't find one. "Sorry," I say. "Not a clue."

"Rugby," he says. "A rugby league."

Then he shows me how he has divided the creatures on
each of his shelves the way a dedicated coach would organize
a rugby team, with the slow, heavy ogres playing the scrum
half; the dinosaurs on the wing; the faster, more martial
knights in the fly half; and the wizards in place as team
captains. "I pit them against each other, and play out entire
league competitions. All in my mind, of course," he says.

All in his mind is how he dealt with the realities of the
Army, for which he had no great love. In fact, throughout
his year of service, he kept a running total of precisely how
many seconds he had left until his discharge.

We were on a particularly brutal four-hour, ten-mile, night stretcher march, the longest one we had ever done till then. Lieutenant Eli, who had some crazy notion he was honoring Paul and Danno because they had been chosen to take a medic's course, decided that our platoon would carry two loaded stretchers instead of the one that other platoons carried. This meant that we had to spend twice the amount of time helping with the stretchers before we could switch off. On top of that, the two "pilots," Jake and David, the guys riding the stretchers, were two of our heaviest men.

At each set of handles, front and back, there are two sets of guys of about the same height, to divide the weight equally. My partner was Brian. After half an hour, I was exhausted, but when I looked over at Brian I saw that he wasn't even breathing hard. Two hours later, I was ready to drop. I could feel my leg muscles shredding with every step. What infantrymen call "the home of the stretcher," the place on my shoulder where the stretcher rested, had a two-inch gouge in it.

I was not the only one suffering. Guys on all sides of us were whimpering or cursing under their breath in Spanish, English, or Afrikaans. Avi, a short, powerful Chilean marching in front of me, was squealing, "Somebody . . . somebody please take the jerry can." I knew how he felt. A filled jerry can weighs twenty-two pounds, but it isn't the weight alone that makes carrying it so uncomfortable. The problem is that it rests on your shoulder higher than the stretcher handle so there's no way to get comfortable under it.

"Somebody . . . somebody . . ." whimpered Avi.

"I've got it," said Brian, relieving Avi of the jerry can. Brian was not even sweating.

As we approached the last half hour of the march, my teeth were sore from gritting them against the pain. My stomach muscles were knotted from the effort I was making to hold back my tears, and I was searching the side of the

road for the right ditch into which I could collapse. And still
the lights of the base receded toward the horizon. Beside me,
the unflappable Brian marched, his eyes looking straight
ahead, his face expressionless, as he carried Avi's jerry can
on his shoulder.

Finally, I could stand it no longer. "How the hell do you
do it?" I groaned. "Why aren't you hurting like the rest of
us?"

"How can I?" he said. "I'm Ironman."

Ironman. The comic book Ironman, who is really Tony
Stark the engineer, who designed a space-age exoskeleton
for himself which he puts on each time he goes off to fight
evil.

Bitterly I asked, "Why not Superman?" I mean, if you're
going to invoke a superhero, why not go all the way?

Brian shifted the jerry can. "Naaah. I'm saving him for
the beret march."

I wasn't as close to the guys from the South American or
European tents as I was to my fellow Americans. My high
school French had left me long ago and I had no Spanish.
We got on together as best we could with various combina-
tions of Hebglish, Franish, and with Mario, Bruce Springsteen lyrics.

Language, in any case, is not really a barrier. I found
ways to get on well with Avi, the Jewish/Vietnamese/Chil-
ean who left Chile for a new life in Israel, and just as well
with Gilli, a short, curly-headed soccer player from Argentina who was promised a tryout with Maccabee Tel Aviv, a
professional soccer team, after the Army.

The guys I know best in the European tent are both Pari-
sians. There is Josh, our expert on water-canteen discipline
and the Samba, and André, our tall, handsome eighteen-
year-old.

The South Africans are the *aleph-aleph*, the crackerjack

soldiers of the outfit. I don't recall any of them ever getting into trouble, except James, our medic, who once had a grass-hopper jump out of his firing chamber when he presented his gun for inspection.

Theirs is always the first tent ready for inspection each morning. They turn out so fast that I wonder sometimes if they don't actually sleep on top of their made beds beside their rolled-up sleeping bags. I know that they fill up a water container every evening so they can mop the floor in a hurry before morning inspection.

The Americans are a pragmatic bunch. We get up promptly but not enthusiastically. We work quietly and me-thodically and are always finished just in time for inspection. The Europeans spend the morning bickering and are some-times ready on time. As for the South Americans—they clearly don't want to get up. Period.

These are the guys I'm with. Here we are somewhere in the middle of the country and it's raining. We've worked well together and we've established a certain amount of trust. I like a lot of these guys and yet—

I wonder now if that will be enough. At the end of this week, we will have finished two thirds of our basic training, and in the eyes of the Army, we will be combat-ready soldiers, ready to be mobilized in case of need. And in Israel there is usually need.

Who knows. For now, the sound of the rain on the tents soothes me to sleep.

The end of one wet day in the Army.

7

On November 15, a twenty-two-year-old yeshiva student was stabbed to death in the Old City of Jerusalem by three Arabs from Jenin, who were immediately arrested. The murder and the arrests set off a week of rioting and counter-rioting by Jewish and Arab residents of the Old City. Several Arab apartments were set on fire by gasoline bombs, and house and car windows were smashed.

The yeshiva where the youth studied asked for, and was given, permission for a demonstration on Saturday evening to mark the end of the seven-day mourning period. The demonstration, involving thousands of Orthodox and right-wing nationalist Jews, will take place on the spot in the Moslem Quarter where the student was killed.

Our company is being sent from its field training to the Old City for the weekend where we will be part of a force of hundreds of policemen and soldiers that will do its best to keep the peace of Jerusalem.

We load up our equipment on trucks, and as I settle in on the bus with only my rifle and *ephod,* a thought strikes me.

I'm on my way to my first professional action as a soldier in the Israeli Army and I don't know if I will be confronting Arabs or Jews.

We arrive at the base in Jerusalem where we will spend the weekend, and after organizing our gear in our rooms, we are called into the dining area, where a colonel from the Border Guard briefs us.

The Border Guard is the police military branch responsible for keeping the peace in sensitive areas of Israel proper, as well as in the "administered territories"—the West Bank and Gaza Strip. The Guard has a high percentage of Druze Arabs, who are Israeli citizens and do national service in its Army. Most of the rest are Arabic-speaking Jews.

The colonel's briefing is lengthy and I will hear one or another version of it so many times during my service that I will know it by heart:

"The Holy Places of Jerusalem are sacred to the local population and absolutely off limits to you . . . All questioning or arrests should cause as little trouble and call as little attention to the event as possible . . . Violating a woman's honor in any way is an unforgivable offense in Arab culture and we respect that. You should never act in any way that is insulting to a woman. You may not touch her, even to arrest her . . .

"Remember, too, that though you are armed you are allowed to fire your weapons only if your life or the lives of innocent civilians are in clear and immediate danger. Any shooting serves to inflame an already tense situation and is counter to our goals. So don't shoot if you can help it."

To emphasize these points, our NCOs pass out pocket-size cards with these and other "Security Guidelines" to keep with us for handy reference.

Next, we are divided into our working units. Every two or three trainees will work with a squad leader from the Border

Guard. I have the rest of the day free on the base but tomorrow, Saturday, I will work all day. There is no Sabbath when we're on duty. And finally, we are on duty.

Saturday morning I eat a quick breakfast of yogurt, a hard-boiled egg, and a fresh roll; stand for a quick inspection of my rifle, magazines, helmet, and *ephod;* jump in the back of a truck; and am off to the Old City with dozens of other soldiers. We're working on the 6 A.M. to 4 P.M. shift. Then we'll break for dinner and come back at 6 P.M. The demonstration is scheduled for 8 P.M., shortly after sundown, and we'll work until there's quiet. We're told it may be a long night.

I'm teamed up with Bill, the burly MAGist from Washington, D.C., and Avi, from Chile. Bill has left his MAG on the base and will patrol with a Galil, like the rest of us. A sergeant from the Border Guards climbs over to us, jostled by the motion of the truck, and introduces himself as Ya'akov, our squad leader for the morning. He's a man of average height, blue eyed, with sandy blond hair worn longer than the usual army length. Though he's obviously an Ashkenazi, he's fluent in Arabic. He tells us that our duties will consist mainly of a foot patrol from the Damascus Gate through the Moslem Quarter along El-Wad Road, a main street since Roman times, past the Via Dolorosa into the heart of the Old City toward the Western Wall and the Jewish Quarter. Then we'll bear right up El-Shilshela to David Street, where I used to look for additions to my coin collection, then on toward the Armenian Quarter and Jaffa Gate. Ya'akov shows us the route on the map and gives us the frequency and code names for the walkie-talkie he carries.

"Any questions?" he asks. We're just pulling into Dung Gate.

I've got one. "Sargeant Ya'akov?"

He winces. "Ya'akov. Just Ya'akov." He's at the tail end

of his service and doesn't give a damn that our commanders still insist on full army protocol.

"OK, Ya'akov. How do you think it'll be today?"

"Ein lecha ma lid'og," he answers. Loosely translated, that's "Piece of cake."

Our truck pulls up to the square next to the Western Wall and disgorges its load.

The hundreds of Orthodox Jews at their Sabbath prayers hardly notice the sound that dozens of pairs of combat boots make striking the pavement or the sharp clicks as we check our weapons once, twice, to see that there is no bullet in the chamber. Their Sabbath reverie is no more disturbed by the clicks of our magazines being slipped into place than they are by the not too dissimilar sound of the clicking tourist cameras behind them.

Watching them sway, I remember passing a synagogue on another street in Jerusalem on another Sabbath—Yom Kippur, 1973. Even then, with air raid sirens going and Arab armies attacking on two fronts, these Orthodox Jews went through the sequence of their prayers all the way to the final shofar blast, oblivious to the chaos around them.

It's a short walk to El-Wad Road, where we do a final radio check and start our patrol. We walk behind Ya'akov the way we've been taught—staggered formation each soldier several feet from the next, his right hand on the grip of his gun, rifle barrel and eyes moving in synch. I'm the last guy in line. Bill, directly in front of me, turns every few seconds to check on me, and I, in turn, spin from time to time and look behind me—just in case.

As we approach the Damascus Gate, Ya'akov turns and notices our deadly, intent manner. He smiles and calls us over.

"Look," he says, "Today *is* tense. By all means keep your

eyes open, especially in doorways and on rooftops. But remember, this is Jerusalem, not Beirut. Take it a little easy."

After fifteen minutes at the Damascus Gate, I feel as if I'm in a game of who's watching whom. I watch the Jews going to the Western Wall, the Moslems on their way to the Al Aqsa Mosque, the Christians going to the Holy Sepulchre. They are all being watched by the tourists from Europe, Asia, Africa, and the Americas. Beggars, merchants, and money traders watch the tourists, hoping for handouts or a little business. And there we are, the soldiers watching them all.

When someone comes by who is "suspicious-looking," an arbitrary category defined today by Ya'akov, who has the most experience, we call the suspect over for a check. Two soldiers look at his identity card while the other two cover the interrogation from a few feet away. Although there are things to look for both on the card and on a suspect's face, arrests are rare. Mostly we are just making our presence felt. Ideally, our being there and asking questions should be enough to intimidate and flush out anyone who is really looking to make trouble.

Ya'akov stops a guy every few minutes and we trainees alternate questioning the suspect with Ya'akov and covering from the side. When it is Avi's turn to question, he says, "No. You do it. I'll stand cover for you."

"Why, what's up?" I ask.

"I just don't want to do it." His face is firmly set. His eyes seem darker than usual. "OK," I say. I join Ya'akov while Avi and Bill cover us.

Later I ask Avi, "What's the problem, hey? Come on, we've got to work together. You've got to tell us what's bugging you."

Bill is next to me and Ya'akov has come over too.

After a couple of false starts, Avi tells us. "Look. I've been through all this at home. But in Chile I was the guy on the other end, getting hassled for my ID. It's one of the reasons I left. I just don't want to make anyone feel like I felt, that's all."

Ya'akov says, "No problem, Avi. Just cover us, all right? We'll do the questioning."

"Yeah. OK, fine," Avi replies. But I can see that the issue is far from resolved in his mind.

We get on with the work but Avi remains tense, preoccupied. As we walk through the streets of the Old City, I smell the *za'atar* and *sahleb* and remember these streets from another time. My coin dealer has long since moved on, but the Christian Arab family that owns the dress shop where my mother was a frequent customer is still there. Although we were all on good terms when we last saw each other, I don't go in to say hello.

The tourists love us. We are constantly being asked to pose for pictures. "Yeah, that's it. Stand there next to my wife. Can you hold the gun out in front? Great, now smile." As we pass a group of pilgrims from Minnesota and Wisconsin, I overhear the Israeli tour guide talking about us. "You can tell by their red boots that they are paratroopers, some of the best soldiers in the Army." I turn and flash them my best all-American-boy smile and throw in a Midwestern "You betcha!" for good measure.

In fact, between the smells and the memories and the tourists, I am almost having a good time. Almost, but every few minutes Ya'akov motions another Palestinian kid over to us for questioning and suddenly the mood changes. I watch the kids walk over, each one trying not to look too scared or too defiant. And for the most part, they're neither. They've been stopped and questioned dozens of times before and are used to the routine, used to showing their identity cards. In short, they're used to being young, male, and Arab in a Jewish state.

We make one arrest. A Palestinian about twenty years old,

dressed in the dusty blue pants and workshirt of a laborer. He has no ID and that's illegal. Everyone in Israel—Jew and Arab alike—is required to carry an identification card. He says that he's left it at home. A friend who is with him goes to call his sister so she can bring the ID card to the Police Station near Jaffa Gate, where he will be kept until she comes. As we make the the long walk to the Jaffa Gate, all eyes turn toward us—a young Arab worker surrounded by four armed soldiers. The Arab men who see us shake their heads. The women make a clucking sound at us that means "Shame, shame."

We drop the kid off and walk back to the Damascus Gate. I'm keeping one eye on each suspect and one eye on Avi. I don't like how quiet he's become and I don't like the fact that each time we question a suspect, Avi stands closer and closer as he provides cover.

It's almost 4 P.M., break time. Ya'akov spots one final suspect and signals me to join him in the questioning. Avi stops me with a movement of his hand and walks in front of me and then in front of Ya'akov. Bill and I are surprised but we cover him.

"Allo, you there!" Avi shouts. "Yeah, you. Come over here. Where are you from? Yeah? Where are you going? What's in the sack? *Jible hawiye,* let's see your identity card . . ."

After a boxed dinner brought from the base and eaten quickly in an alleyway, we are reassigned to Sergeant Bassam, who is to be our squad leader for the duration of the demonstration. He is a large, pleasant Druse from the town of Daliat-al-Carmel near Haifa. We're neighbors, he and I, and I've been there on occasional Saturdays for shopping and lunch. The Druse villages on the Carmel mountain range are the few places near my kibbutz where stores are open on the Sabbath.

Bassam, too, refuses to be called "Sergeant." Like Ya'akov, he's near the end of his service, although he's been asked to become an officer and is thinking of signing on for the extra time.

We continue our patrols with him, only this time we concentrate on the area around the narrow intersection in the Moslem Quarter where the Jewish demonstration will take place. We check alleyways, doorways, and rooftops for suspicious objects. Over the course of the day we've heard reports on the walkie-talkie of occasional stones being thrown from rooftops, but so far no one's been hurt. Police raids earlier in the day on both Jewish and Arab homes in the area have netted Molotov cocktails. Some arrests have been made.

About six-thirty we get a report that a Molotov cocktail has been thrown at one of our patrols several streets from us. We run full speed to where it happened and find several soldiers from Platoon 1 of my company looking shaken as they guard six suspects who have their hands up against an iron doorway. The air is heavy with the acrid smell of burnt gasoline, and glass is strewn everywhere. Lieutenants Eli and Ehud are already on the scene directing the search for anything or anybody suspicious. Mahlouf, a mean-spirited Moroccan trainee from Platoon 1, stands directly behind the suspects, who are all in their late teens. If any of them turns around or moves too much, Mahlouf bangs the offender's head hard against the metal shutters to remind him to stay still.

Nothing else is found, and after brief questioning by Border Guard officers, the suspects are released. Because of my English, Lieutenant Ehud drafts me into service as press liaison to explain the scene to the reporters who have gathered at the end of the block. I'm pleased at this opportunity for public service and think out a detailed, yet concise account of the Incident of the Molotov Cocktail. But the reporters, who have had more experience in these situations than

I, are already moving on to find good places from which to watch the demonstration which is about to begin. Frustrated, I find Bassam and we, too, take our places.

The Jewish demonstrators will march to the site on El-Wad Road where the student was killed. It is the same street we've been patrolling all day and it is lined on both sides by police, Border Guards, and soldiers. Behind us are reporters and curious onlookers. I'm standing between Bassam and Bill at a turn in the road. Avi stands next to Bill. Our immediate goal is to keep the marchers, who have have been calling for revenge all week, separated from the local Arabs.

Over Bassam's radio comes the announcement, "Demonstrators approaching." Then I hear a distant sound increase rapidly in volume until it becomes fully tumultuous. A noise that earlier had sounded like distant bells ringing is now heard for what it is: the crashing noise of sticks banging against the metal shutters of the closed shops. The marchers are chanting, "Revenge. We want revenge. Revenge. We want revenge."

One of the reporters who had rebuffed my explanation of the Molotov cocktail incident earlier nudges me from behind and asks, "What're they chanting?"

"Peace, love, freedom, happiness," I answer. The reporter nods and writes.

Just then, an Arab girl of about twelve pushes her way between Bassam and me into the street. She is carrying schoolbooks and has on the green uniform of one of the local religious schools. The first phalanx of the marchers is upon us; the Arab girl's shriek is muffled as she is engulfed by the crowd yelling for revenge in a language she does not know.

The marchers are hatred in motion. I see the fire of it in their eyes, hear the hoarse sound of it in their voices as they call for vengeance. Some are Orthodox Jews wearing skull caps or broad hats and black suits. Others are more casually dressed in shirts and slacks. Here and there I can see the yellow T-shirt of Meir Kahane's violence-prone Kach party.

As they sweep by, the marchers are at first not quite sure what to make of this schoolgirl in their midst, who by now has dropped her books and has her hands to her face as she stands paralyzed with terror.

"Come on," says Bassam. The four of us, Bassam, Bill, Avi, and I, move into the melee and surround the girl, much as we surrounded the ID-less suspect earlier. The crowd jostles us but we're able to move with the girl to the outer edge of the melee.

Bassam crouches down. "Where do you live?" he asks the girl. She may be suspicious of the uniform but she responds to the fluent Arabic and the soothing tone.

"*Hunak,* over there," she answers, and points in the direction across the street where the stream of chanting demonstrators is still flowing by.

"No good. Do you know somebody else who lives over that way?" He points in the opposite direction, away from the crowd. "An uncle or an aunt, maybe."

She nods, and in doing so, wipes the tears from her cheek.

We walk with her to a house a short distance away and knock on the door. The woman who answers, an older, heavyset woman wearing a traditional Arab dress and red plastic sandals, looks scared when she sees four soldiers at her door. Then she is puzzled when she notices her niece. Bassam explains the situation to her and suggests that the girl spend the evening there instead of trying to make it home.

"Better keep your door and shutters locked for the next little while," he adds, as we turn to leave.

"*Shukran,* thank you," the aunt calls after us as she closes and bolts her door. "*Shukran awi,* thank you very much."

We return to the corner where we had been. I see that the shutters of the stores along the street have held up to the blows of the demonstrators, and except for the odd broken window, there is little to mark the hateful wave that washed by earlier. Then I see the torn, dirty pages and broken spine of what was once the little girl's Arabic textbook.

The formal part of the demonstration passes uneventfully. Once the politicians and religious leaders start making speeches, the crowd calms down. But when the speeches are over, the crowd breaks into small gangs who patrol the streets and alleys looking for someplace or someone on whom to vent their anger. We know, too, that there are Arab gangs, frustrated by this Jewish presence, and angry at being kept away from one of their major streets, who are similarly patroling the same streets and alleys looking for a focus for *their* rage. So our task for the rest of the evening will be to patrol the streets ourselves and try to keep the two groups apart. Bill, however, suggests a more pragmatic approach. "Let's just close off the Old City for a few days and let them at each other."

Well after midnight, when we are finally back at the base, we take a survey of the night's damage. Except for several broken windows and a couple of minor injuries from thrown rocks, the damage to the Old City and its residents, Jewish and Arab, has been light. Our company has had only one casualty. André, the Parisian sniper, has been taken to a hospital with a slight concussion from a rock thrown at him when he and the squad he was working with refused to turn over several Arabs they had arrested to a gang of Jews. The Arabs André and his fellow soldiers were protecting had been arrested for throwing rocks.

Tonight, as after all our training exercises, we are debriefed. Lieutenant Ehud says, "You did well. You can be proud of yourselves. There were no deaths and only minor injuries partly because of the way you handled yourselves. With one exception. You, Mahlouf!" He calls out the name of the soldier who had guarded the Arabs suspected of throwing the Molotov cocktail. "I know it's not pleasant to have a gasoline bomb thrown at you. But that uniform you're wearing and the gun you carry don't make you better than anyone else and they certainly don't give you the the right to bang anyone's head against a doorway. You're confined to the base for the next two Saturdays. Company dismissed."

The following Friday, I get a weekend pass. Since I am based near Jerusalem, I decide to give Khalid a call. We lost touch with each other for a while when I came to Israel and he stayed in Berkeley, but he's since come back to Bir Zeit University to finish his degree and we've been able to see each other occasionally.

Arranging a place to meet turns out not to be so simple. Arab East Jerusalem and the Jewish New City were unified in 1967, but after twenty-one years there are still two central bus stations, one on the Nablus Road for buses to Arab towns and the other in Romema that serves Jews. Khalid, coming from Nablus, will arrive in the Arab station while I, when our visit is over, will have to take a bus from the Egged station across town.

Khalid says, "I have a suggestion. You know where the Damascus Gate is . . ."

"Yes," I say. "Oh yes, I do."

Christmas Eve 1986

I feel as if I've walked through a picture. Again, nuns, pilgrims, and dark-suited men from Asia are strolling through Manger Square. Carolers still sing "Silent Night" and "Adeste Fidelis". But this time I'm not in the square with my friend Steve but rather on the rooftop with Jake. We're watching the crowd below for any signs of trouble. For the second time in my life I'm spending Christmas Eve in Bethlehem, but now *we* are the soldiers I looked up and saw when I was here with Steve six years ago.

We've been in Bethlehem for a week preparing for tonight. The Christmas season is a sensitive time because the thousands of pilgrims and tourists make an ideal target for terrorists. The military administration responsible for the West Bank wants to make absolutely sure there is no trouble, so they have had us scouring the hillsides in and around Bethlehem for any weapons or other signs of trouble. And for the first time, and despite the protests of the mayor of Bethlehem, the administration has been sending troops to check all the houses along the main arteries and near Manger Square door to door. Since we arrived, we have progressed from checking identity cards to house-to-house searches.

I work with Sergeant Moshe and five other soldiers. He knocks on a door, and when it is answered, almost invariably by a woman—the men are away at work—he explains in his broken Arabic that we would like to come in and look around. Like the young men whose IDs we checked at the Damascus Gate, these women know what's expected and let us in without trouble.

Moshe and I, as his radioman, and one other soldier go into the house while the other four cover us from outside. The neighborhoods where we conduct our searches are mainly well-to-do. The homes are large, made mostly of Jerusalem stone. Most of the population of Bethlehem is Christian, and we frequently come upon a tile on the archway above the doorway of a Christian home that shows Saint George on horseback driving his lance deep into the bowels of the dragon. Though I stoop, the antenna of my field radio usually bumps St. George, his horse, or the dragon on the nose when I walk under the arch.

The homes are usually clean inside, with the children's sleeping mattresses piled neatly into a closet to give the woman of the house room to work. The ever-present smell of pita baking gets to me as my day progresses and my appetite grows.

We are mostly here to make our presence known, to act as a deterrent to anyone who is looking to make trouble. We have orders to be as polite as possible under the circumstances and we follow those orders, even to excess.

Matti, one of the more liberal of the South Africans, who, themselves are one of the more liberal groups in the platoon, works with Lieutenant Eli, who speaks no Arabic. He asks Matti to explain in English why they are there. His spiel, which I hear about later, goes something like this:

"Hello, we're the Israeli Army. We're very sorry to disturb you but Christmas is coming, and we want to make sure there is no danger to the pilgrims in the area. We realize that this is a bother but we can't avoid it. Would you please allow us into your home to make sure that there is nothing dangerous?"

Now that's not quite the norm, but we all try to be as respectful as possible of other people's space. Unless there are actually bomb parts, Molotov cocktails, or pamphlets on how to destroy the State of Israel, we leave the place alone, touching as little as possible. Throughout the week, we will only confiscate two Army-issue jerry cans and one gas mask that a kid said he found on the hillside.

Even so, not everybody is pleased with this sudden military presence in their homes. People glare at us and once a woman who answers the door refuses to let us in until her son can call her husband from his place of work several blocks away. We do make one arrest—a guy who said the Army had no right to enter his home and backed it up by taking a swing at Moshe.

Now, patrolling on the roof of the Church of the Nativity, I look in on the mass that Steve and I sat through six years

earlier. Through a half-open stained glass window, the same
breath of air wafts both the murmurs of the prayers being
chanted far below us and the warmth of the bodies and the
church. It's well after midnight and it's clear to both Jake
and me that our only battles tonight will be against boredom
and cold. If all goes well, it will be a silent night, indeed.

New Year's Eve 1986
Our platoon is walking through the night as we've done so
often over the last six months. It's a crisp night—not too
cold but too overcast to see the stars. Carrying Moshe's radio, I walk with him at the back of the platoon. It's a short
march, less than six miles on flat ground, and Lieutenant Eli,
in the lead, is keeping a slow, steady pace. We walk on a dirt
path under wide trees and the sound of a nearby brook
accompanies the plodding of our feet.

Moshe is telling me about squad leader's course and the
joys he found in night navigation in the Negev Desert and
the Golan Heights. I tell him of camping trips I used to take
in Yosemite and Point Reyes.

It's an easy march but the loads we are carrying are
heavier than usual. We're told that our goal is to ambush an
imaginary car which will pass by a certain road a little after
midnight. To that end we've got four bombs made from four
jerry cans, each filled with a forty-five-pound mixture of gasoline, diesel fuel, nails, and strips of rubber. We also have
two mines, two RPG grenades, and thousands of rounds of
ammunition.

We get to the road about eleven forty-five and line up
along a ridge overlooking it. In the middle, directly in front
of us, is a three-level pyramid of fifty-gallon drums representing the car we're not supposed to see until midnight. The
bomb and mine bearers creep down to the road and set their
devices. The RPGists and snipers sight in their weapons.
The MAGists, David and Bill, on the flanks, set up their

machine guns and set the first round in the chamber. They have worked for two days putting together belts of 1,000 rounds apiece of nothing but tracer shells. The rest of us click our magazines into our Galils.

Then, at midnight, we get the order, "Fire!"

First, the night lights up as the bombs go off, two on either side of the "car" to close it off. They go off with a tremendous roar of noise and flame punctuated by the flashes of burning rubber being flung out on all sides, and the clink of nails striking the barrels. Then, the two smaller RPG explosions rock us and two of the top barrels fall, each with its own four-inch hole clean through it. Then we all open fire. The MAGists fire from the sides, their tracer shells looking like lasers stabbing the darkness. David doesn't even stop to change his barrel, which soon gets red hot.

About five minutes and thousands of rounds later we get our cease-fire. All the barrels have fallen and they have so many holes they look like they might blow away in the wind.

The way back to base promises to be even easier than the way out, because most of our load has gone up in smoke and fire. Except my load. I'm lugging thirty pounds of field radio. But Tal, who has an empty back, comes over.

"Happy New Year," he says, as he takes the radio from me.

Yeah, I guess. The year seems to have flown by: milking cows, driving tractors, marching, running, firing.

The Immigrant's Guide to Military Service says that basic training serves two purposes:

1) To teach individuals the essentials of soldiering.
2) To teach people from different cultures and walks of life to work together and help one another.

Well, I've sure learned that. Plus, I now know two new phrases in Arabic: *Jible hawiye* and *Iftah el-bab*, which mean respectively, "Give me your identity card," and "Open the door."

"Yeah, Tal," I answer, "Happy New Year."

8

Last night I lay shivering in a two-man tent on the Golan Heights. Now, I'm on El Al's Flight 001 from Tel Aviv to New York. I'm leaning back in a comfortable soft seat in the air-conditioned cabin. The coffee is hot and I can drink as much as I like. The stewardesses are perky and polite. After the *manot krav* I was eating on the Golan, even El Al's airline food tastes good. The farther west I fly, the better the Army looks.

And the better its paternal—nearly maternal—concern for the welfare of its soldiers looks. Because it's the Army's *hayal boded* policy that's sending me back to the States for a month's visit. It's a policy meant to allow the *hayal boded,* "the lone soldier," to maintain family ties. In ordinary cases every soldier is allowed a home visit every two or three weeks for a weekend of his mother's cooking and a bout of listening to his father's stories of his own Army service "back when things were *really* tough." But for the soldier like myself, who does not have family in Israel, the Army tries to arrange an alternative for his weekend passes. Usu-

136

ally, the *hayal boded* is adopted by a kibbutz for the duration of his service, as I have been, or the Army may even subsidize an apartment for him in the city of his choice.

A *hayal boded* is entitled to other benefits as well. Because he has no family in Israel to slip him pocket money from time to time, he has a higher base pay so he can, like his comrades, afford cigarettes, an occasional felafel, or a movie. On weekends he is, in principle, entitled to leave the base earlier so he can get his Sabbath shopping done before the stores close on Friday. And if his family lives abroad, he is entitled (again in principle) to a three-minute phone call home every three months. It is a happy principle, but the realities of active service do not always allow me time to make those calls. In my two years in the Army, I got to make one Army-sponsored call to the States.

Best of all, the *hayal boded* whose immediate family lives abroad has the right once a year (twice during his service) to say goodbye to his friends who are sleeping in the freezing rain or crawling around in the freezing mud of the Golan Heights, salute his sergeants, hop on a bus to his kibbutz where he can store his army clothes, and dressed in civilian clothing, make his way to Ben Gurion Airport for El Al Flight 001 bound for New York, family, and thirty days of good manners, indoor plumbing, and as many Snickers bars as he can eat.

The sun is setting on the left side of the plane as the second of two groups of Hassidim goes to the rear of the aircraft to say *Ma'ariv,* their late evening prayers. An earlier group, unable to agree with this bunch about when the sun was due to set, calculated for our westward travel, has already finished praying.

I fidget in my seat, trying to get comfortable enough to sleep, but the Hadassah matron from Rochester, New York, sitting beside me is full of the miracle of Israel, and wants to tell me all about it.

She seems to be in her mid-fifties, with permanent-waved gray hair. A tall, handsome woman who could pass for TV's Bea Arthur, she wears a huge gold *chai* suspended from a gold chain on her neck and four rings, two gold, two diamond, on her left hand. She is going home after two weeks in Israel.

"It's my fifth trip. By now I feel almost like a sabra. And those young Israelis. How alive they are. How vibrant. Life is so different for them than for our young people. Everything's so real.

"And I still get the same thrill every time I see the Wall or spend Shabbat in Tsfat. It's so exciting."

Listening to her, I think, "I hope it doesn't get too exciting." Because the rumor, just before I left my base, is that our company will be doing border patrol in Lebanon.

For the longest time, the lady from Rochester is oblivious to the crutches resting between our seats and the cumbersome cast on my left leg. Her comment, when she does notice it, is so American that it, more than the flight listing back at Ben Gurion, more even than the captain's trilingual announcement, lets me know that we are on our way back to the United States. All last week, any Israeli noting my age and the cast on my leg asked the obvious question, "Training accident?" or sometimes, "Parachute jump?"

But this sweet motherly woman from Rochester, easing me back into the Western Hemisphere, asks, "Oh, ski accident?"

Well, in a way.

Just three weeks ago, I'm with my company as it sets out one night with the other basic trainees on a ten-hour, forty-mile jog/walk. When we complete it, we will have the right to wear the black beret.

The route is comparatively flat as we skirt the citrus groves south of our base. There is no night discipline on beret marches so we're moving along singing, sometimes with each other, sometimes with whatever songs are coming out of the boom box.

Though the discipline is easy and we don't have to carry a guy on a stretcher, there are several things that make the march hard: First, this will be the longest march we've done so far, and I'm not the only one who is wondering if I'll make it to the end. Then, Lieutenant Ehud, our company commander, intent on keeping up *his* standards of excellence, has started us off at a gruelling five-miles-per-hour pace, which exhausts us almost before we've begun. It's a psychologically shrewd move on his part, because when, two hours into the march, he lets us slow to four miles per hour, we are so relieved we feel we can maintain this strolling pace all night long. As in fact, we do. Finally, it's raining. And raining. When, for a moment, the rain lets up, it starts to hail. One way or another, this march of ours turns out to to be Israel's wettest night of the year.

We are grateful to the rain for cooling the night, but we are not happy about the mud through which we have to slog, or about the raging torrents that, at intervals, we are required to cross.

As the radioman for our platoon, I am supposed to be walking behind Lieutenant Ehud so that I can hand him the headset whenever he needs it. Now he needs it, but he's outstripped me and I have to put on a burst of steam to catch up with him. Finally, and with some help from the other guys, who push me forward, I catch up just as he plunges into one of those torrents and reaches back for the handset. Attached to him by the phone line, I follow him into the water where, in midstream, my left leg sinks into the mud and gets stuck. Lieutenant Ehud, meanwhile, has reached firmer ground and starts to speed up.

Caught between the force he exerts by pulling on the line, and the power of the river's current pushing me downstream, I find my mired leg being twisted. As I struggle to maintain my balance, I have a swift memory of a high school physics class in which I learned about torque and moment, and then my leg is flooded with pain.

An observation frequently repeated during our training is that your body knows when it has had enough. "If something is really wrong, you'll pass out. Otherwise, keep going." So, since I have not passed out, I keep going, though I do call Nathan, who is behind me, to take the radio from me. Then I tell Rafi, the company medic, who is marching nearby, "Hey, I think something's wrong with my leg. It hurts."

"Of course it hurts," he says. "You're halfway through a forty-mile march. What do you expect?"

A little sympathy maybe, but never mind. We finish the march and return to the base in record time while my leg keeps sending signals of distress. After breakfast, a shower, and a couple of hours sleep, we are marched onto the parade ground where, in a simple ceremony, the base commander presents us with our black berets. It's a proud moment, but my leg continues to complain.

"My leg hurts," I tell the doctor on the base.

"Of course it hurts. You finished a forty-mile march last night. What do you expect?"

The weeks go by, but the pain in my leg does not fade. We spend our days cleaning the base and rehearsing for our graduation from basic training. Then one day, we graduate and are transferred to the Such-and-Such Battalion of the Nahal brigade for advanced training and border patrol. A new base and a new doctor. I take my complaining leg to him.

Medical care in the Israeli army is generally good. Israeli combat medicine, especially its Medical Evacuation Units

and frontline psychiatrists, are world-renowned, the former
for daring rescues of behind-the-lines wounded, the latter for
expeditious treatment of battle fatigue at the front. However,
if you're not actually at a front, or if you happen not to have
battle fatigue, you may have a problem. Base doctors are
likely to be reservists who have been selected from a pool of
physicians with all sorts of medical specialties. In my case,
the doctor to whom I bring my complaining leg is a gynecol-
ogist.

"According to your records, you've complained about this
leg a lot. What are you, a *tachman,* a shirker?" asks Captain
Dr. Levy, Ob-Gyn.

"No, sir. It hurts."

"Of course it hurts. You're an infantryman. Their legs
always hurt."

"But sir . . ."

"All right," he grumbles. "I'll send you to x-ray. Fast, so
you can be out and running again by tonight."

I watch the orthopedist as he studies the x-ray he has just
made of my leg. "So," he says. "It hurts, does it?"

"Yes, sir," I answer, my heart sinking once again.

"Of course it hurts." Here it comes. "Of course it hurts.
It's broken. Looks like it's been broken for the past couple
of weeks. I'll have a cast on it within the hour."

Great. A month with a cast and crutches would make
another soldier the envy of the platoon. A month at home
except for occasional visits to a recuperation clinic where
he'd be helped along by sweet and caring nurses. A month of
telling tall stories about how he broke his leg.

But my month to recuperate coincides with my *hayal
boded* leave of absence to visit my family. On that trip I was
planning to do some ice skating, and maybe a little scuba
diving.

Well, at least I'll have to pack only one shoe.

———

From my vantage point on crutches, I discover that civilization has a smell. A clean smell of endless boxes of Snickers bars in a New York supermarket. Snickers bars about which I had dreamed in my tent on the wet slopes. Hershey bars, M & M's, rows of wonderful things: canned peaches, fruit cocktail, pyramids of Nescafé jars. Restaurants everywhere perfectly willing to serve you coffee with milk five times, ten times, twenty times a day.

And there are civilians. Just people, not in uniform, who are not being ordered to do anything that would keep them cold and wet. Who are not wondering if they will end up doing duty on the West Bank or in Lebanon. And they are American civilians, which means that they smile and say "thank you." Even New Yorkers.

And while I drink the coffee, I read the New York *Times,* in which bad things happen "out there."

But it's things like the coffee and the paper that bring up my other feelings. On Valentine's Day, I read about the Israeli Navy off the coast of Lebanon stopping a boat with fifty Fatah terrorists aboard. The news triggers an impulse in me to get back to Israel. Much as I love my friends and family in the States, I find myself missing my Israeli world: my kibbutz "family," the guys in my unit. In the land of freshly ground coffee, I find myself missing the taste of Moshe's Nescafé after a hard exercise. I even miss Tommy's solar tea. What I don't miss, not at all, not even a little bit, is the Army training itself, the nightmare *imun mitkadem,* advanced training, from which I was plucked because of my broken leg.

January 3, 1987

Dear Mom and Dad,
I really don't have time to write a real letter—we're at the tail end of what's called "the Big Exercise" (good

fighters, lousy imagery), the culmination of all we've learned in basic training. What that really means is six weeks of maneuvers, tents, rain, fatigue, hunger—all the glories of army life.

Anyway, back to it. On Wednesday, we have our final march for our black berets. Forty miles with seventy pounds on our backs. I suppose we could buy our berets in the PX, but there's more honor doing it this way.

Love,

A.

P.S. This lay on my desk for three weeks until I came home to the kibbutz again. We made the march in the year's worst storm: rain, hail, mud. Next time I head to the PX.

We're off now for advanced training in the Golan Heights. I'll let you know how it goes.

A.

The Golan Heights is a basaltic plateau that rises sharply 3,000 feet above the Hula Valley and the Sea of Galilee. The rocky ground makes for difficult walking and dangerous running. The steepness of the terrain was of particular strategic importance to the Syrians, who controlled them from 1948 until 1967. They were equally important to the Israelis, who took them after fierce fighting in 1967 and defended them at great cost in 1973. Because of their strategic value, Israel all but annexed the Heights in 1982, applying Israeli law to the region.

The weather in the Golan is both variable and harsh. At 3,000 feet, the temperature is at least ten degrees cooler than the valley below. In the winter months, the thermometer can dip below freezing. And the north-south alignment of the plateau means that every storm system carried westward by the jet stream will dump its load on the Golan. Usually that means rain, but it can also mean hail and even snow. Whichever, it is always cold or wet.

We arrive at the temporary base of the Such-and-Such Battalion of the Nahal Brigade and we know immediately that we're in for changes. Unlike our permanent base for basic training, this temporary base is meant to be moved often and is built to be taken apart quickly. There are no permanent buildings. No concrete floors. No showers or bathrooms. All we see are tents. Tents for the soldiers (one tent per platoon), tents for the officers and NCOs. Tents for company supplies and for the company office. There is a tent for the clinic, one for the armory, and one for the kitchen.

The first thing we do is prepare our equipment. Because we signed off on our old equipment at our basic training base, we must now get our new personal gear and *pakalim* into battle-ready condition. That means getting our packs, our belts, our straps, and our helmets in good shape. Now we see how training pays off. The work that took us several weeks to do when we were in basic now takes three days. Of course, to accomplish this we don't sleep.

At the end of the second day, our work is subject to inspection: sergeant inspection, first-sergeant inspection, and platoon commander's inspection. It is only after we have been given Lieutenant Eli's detailed critique of our performance that we can really get to work.

Our tent is a mess. There are coils of rope and scraps of plastic sheeting everywhere. Mario has been reissued an M203 grenade launcher. Through the dust and haze of my own exhaustion, I watch him from across the tent where he is jerry-rigging quick-release sleeves for his grenade pack using strips of innertubes and plastic ties. I vaguely see him melting the ends of plastic strips with a candle. Some part of my mind registers that the candle flame is also lapping against the head of an antipersonnel grenade. The words "candle," "flame," and "grenade" stir in my mind. There is meaning here, and slowly it reaches me. I stumble over the cots and bodies of other guys working on their equipment and drop down beside Mario.

"Hey, buddy. How about we move this over here," I suggest, as I slip the grenade out of its rubber sleeve and away from the flame.

"Oh, yeah," he says, sounding as tired as I am. "Yeah, you've got a point."

Now we have company commander's inspection. Lieutenant Ehud is his usual thorough self, checking every detail of every piece of equipment. Finally, he pronounces us ready for Battalion Commander's inspection. When Lieutenant Colonel Y., the battalion commander, comes into our tent, he seems barely to notice our gear neatly laid out on our bunks. He and Lieutenant Ehud exchange pleasantries, then he turns to us and says, "Good work. In the last three days, you and the rest of the battalion have moved from nothing to full combat preparedness. Congratulations. Now, get to work."

This is where the next three months of advanced training will take place. Here is where we will put in the two-week transition period of training known as the *gibbush*, the consolidation. What it means is that we will be worked so hard that, for the sake of survival, we will learn to work together —so well that we will become a cohesive unit.

There is an expression that's popular in the Israeli Army: "Hard training makes easy combat." The idea is to make training just as hard as possible so that you'll be prepared for anything in combat. To that end, we are driven endlessly to the limits of our endurance and beyond. We learn that we *can* go three days without sleep; that we *can* go two days without eating; that we *can* march thirty, forty, fifty miles if we have to.

And that's what advanced training, and especially the *gib-bush,* is about.

If we had four or five hours of sleep per night during basic training, now we are lucky to get two hours. Two hours, that is, if we don't count the half-hour interruption most nights for guard duty. At any break in an exercise, we plop down for a few minutes rest. Sometimes, though my hands are freezing, I find I'm too tired to put them in my pockets.

We are perpetually on our feet on exercises. These are similar in principle to those we did in basic training, but they are more intricate and on a larger scale. The smallest unit we work in now is the company and sometimes it can be as large as a battalion.

Sometimes we work alongside tanks: Centurion M60s or the new Israeli-built Merkavas. We learn, too, to work with helicopters: the attack Bell 209 Cobras, the Hughes Defenders, the Bell 212 troop carriers, and the larger Sikorsky CH53s.

My first few rides in a helicopter, when the roar of blades and the surging power of takeoffs are still new, feel tremendously exciting, but once the novelty wears off, a helicopter ride turns into just one more opportunity for a catnap.

Exercises seem always to be taking place at night and in the rain. And invariably, they begin with a long march as the platoon moves off to practice a sneak attack somewhere twelve miles away. We move in night formation, and despite the downpour, we don't wear rain gear because all it does is trap our body moisture so that we risk getting heat stroke. So we march without it and learn to accept getting wet, though it takes a while. On my first march, I do what I can to keep my socks dry, but when I walk through water that reaches to my knees, I decide that at least I'll keep my shirt dry. When half an hour later my shirt is soaked, I concentrate on keeping a small patch of cloth under my backpack dry. When the rain rolling off my helmet gets to that, I think, "Well, anyway, my jockey shorts are still dry." Minutes later I walk through a waist-deep stream and just resign myself to being wet.

What I don't resign myself to is growing a beard. The life we lead now is about as low on the scale of evolution as you can get. We're dirty. We sleep in mud, or in soaked pup tents pitched in mud. We eat ghastly food out of tin cans with our fingers. We are wet and cold and so tired we stumble when we walk. In the midst of it all, some of the guys ask for and are given permission to grow beards. This saves them about six minutes preparation time for morning inspection. But I don't. Though in other respects I have accepted the general squalor, I find that I can't (or don't want to) give up the little ritual of shaving. I need it to remind myself I'm human. To look into my little hand mirror and see a face that, for the next little while, will look somewhat civilized. Still, as the weather gets colder, I learn how to soap, lather, and shave with one hand.

This kind of life is not for everyone. Especially not for Platoon 1.

Here in advanced training, we've been working much more closely with the guys in Platoons 1 and 2. If a high school chess club were to form a *garin* and join the Army, they would end up being Platoon 2. To a man, it is made up of bright, slight, gawky guys who, if they were wearing white Oxford shirts, would button them to the top and carry twelve sharpened pencils in a plastic holder in their shirt pockets. They look like they would be more comfortable pushing the buttons on a Hewlett-Packard programmable calculator than pulling the trigger of a Galil assault rifle. But despite their looks, their sense of ideology and commitment is strong, and basic training has forged them into a cohesive fighting unit.

Platoon 1, on the other hand, is made up of guys who were combative before they got into the Army. They are not the sort of people who generally inspire confidence, coming as they do from inner cities and development towns where they have been gang members, thugs, and petty thieves. The Army, however, has seen potential in them and has undertaken to channel their natural fighting instincts. They have been put in uniform and subjected to army discipline. And for a time, just as long as they weren't being pushed too hard, they proved to be reasonably dependable soldiers.

In the *gibbush* on the Golan Heights, they were pushed too hard. After the first week of hiking in rain and sleeping in mud, the entire platoon decided they were tired of being yelled at, tired of being cold, and tired of being tired. They just didn't want to be there any more. So they left. Every last man of Platoon 1 went AWOL. Even Boaz, who was at the dentist when his friends walked off the base, followed after them when he came back to an empty tent.

A couple of hours after they left the base, Lieutenant Itzik, their commanding officer, and Lieutenant Ehud found them eating humous and felafel in a nearby restaurant, but when the officers went out to their jeep to call for a bus to transport them back to the base, every one of them went out the back door of the restaurant. Then, using the night movement tactics they had learned in basic training, they slipped past the range of Lieutenant Ehud's searchlight. When they returned to base a couple of days later, some of them were sent to jail and the rest were confined for a couple of weeks in their tents behind barbed wire.

As we slosh through the mud on the way to our exercises, they wave to us from inside their dry tents. Even though they are behind barbed wire, it's hard to believe that they are the ones being punished.

Though the work and the weather make our lives more difficult, one aspect gets easier: there is less stress on discipline and punishment. We aren't running around bathrooms any-

more. By passing through basic, we have earned our right to
be here. We have our black berets. That means an almost
immediate easing up of harsh language. The mood of the
training changes as we feel ourselves becoming a team, and
the change is signaled loud and clear. At the end of one of
our long marches, we stand drawn up in formation, expecting who knows what sort of dressing-down. Lieutenant Ehud
does indeed analyze our march (everything we ever do is
analyzed when it's over), but as he finishes his talk he says,
"One last thing, soldiers. From now on, when you talk to me,
remember my name is Ehud. And these," he says, pointing
to them, "are Eli and Moshe."

After the *gibbush,* just as we're starting to get used to our
new training schedule, two things happen that take me out of
the routine. The first is that I've finally persuaded a doctor to
let me get the pain I've had in my leg since the beret march
looked at. The second: it's my month to go abroad.
    I'm heartbroken.

April 1987

When I return to my base, it is already spring.
    The muscles in my leg are still weak, so when the com-
pany goes into the field for training, I hobble around helping
Sergeant Moshe clean the camp, make potato pancakes,
French toast, and Nescafé for when the guys return. Slowly,
I work my way back into the routine so that, by the time we
are sent to do border patrol in May, I'll be ready.
    There have been a lot of rumors about our three-month
border patrol assignment, but so far we haven't heard anything concrete. All we know for sure is that we are scheduled
to be sent north. As a result, we listen with special interest to
intelligence reports that the Syrians are only waiting for the
snows to melt to mount an attack on the Golan Heights. In
Lebanon, the Syrians have recently deployed commandos on

the outskirts of Sidon, the farthest south they've been since 1982.

Meanwhile as the weather improves, there is an increase in the number of terrorist attacks along the borders. Several soldiers in the Givati unit patrolling a section of Lebanon known as the Security Strip are killed by booby traps laid by terrorists. In fact, the entire Northern Region is heating up, along with the weather. And there is reason to be concerned about what is still to come because the Palestinian National Council is meeting in Algiers trying to decide how to make its presence felt in the territories on this, the twentieth anniversary of the "occupation."

The word finally comes down: Starting in May, we will be based in the T. region in the center of the Lebanese Security Zone, the same area in which the Givati soldiers had their troubles.

The Security Zone in South Lebanon, the last vestige of Israel's 1982 incursion into Lebanon, is a strip five to ten miles wide. Two years ago, when Israel pulled out of Lebanon after a painful and costly three-year presence, Israel retained access to this strip and fortified it in order to keep Katyusha rockets out of range of her northern settlements and to provide a means of intercepting terrorists before they could get inside Israel's borders.

We, it appears, will be the means.

May 1987

Now I know why the Army uses tents. A day and a half ago, the area where I'm standing was a tent city, a combat battalion center which, under canvas, housed, fed, and supplied hundreds of soldiers. Now it is an empty field where stray cattle from nearby Druse villages nudge the rocks with their noses trying to get at the weeds and wildflowers which grow there.

We are packed and ready to go, but first there are some personnel changes.

Jake, the MAGist from Scarsdale, is also packed, but he's not going to Lebanon with us. Instead, he's on his way back to his kibbutz.

Only a week ago, when Lieutenant Eli scolded Jake for repeatedly missing training exercises, he said in exasperation, "Jake, *ata mevater al atzmecha,* you give up on yourself. One day the habit will catch up with you."

What Lieutenant Eli did not know was that Jake was near the end of his nine-month stint in the Army. So that all that caught up with him were his discharge papers. He is the first member of our platoon to step back into civilian life; he takes his blue down sleeping bag with him.

We have a new platoon member, Manni, a short, bearded Argentinian with a quick smile and an equal passion for Jorge Luis Borges and the music of Muddy Waters. I liked him when I met him on the day of our induction but he was separated from us when the Air Force asked him to volunteer for pilot training. Now, he rejoins us after having spent nine months in that highly competitive program.

The Israeli Army's policy is that it will not send only sons, or those who have lost a close relative, into a combat area unless the soldier gets written permission from his parents. And the permission of the father is not enough. The mother also has to sign the document. What is phenomenal is the way most only sons scramble to get their parents' permission and the frequency with which the parents give it. In our platoon, only Tal is affected. He's already written to South Africa to get his mother's OK.

In the very middle of the excitement of leaving, when we are all packed, our company commander chooses a small group of us to do special detached service in a separate outfit and my platoon goes off without me.

June 1987

Though the work in the unit to which I have been detached is interesting, I begin to lean on Lieutenants Ehud and Eli whenever I see them to send me back to my unit, which by now is actually doing border patrol. I know what's happening from stories in the papers: some of the guys have run into a booby trap and our unit has come under 120-millimeter rocket fire. Sometimes we read about a soldier injured in combat and don't know who he is. And then one evening, as we sit around watching the news, the lead story is that a soldier in the T. region of Lebanon has been killed by a booby trap.

Tobi, the soldier, is not a close friend of mine, but he was a buddy of several of my friends. He was your basic OK guy. Not at all thrilled about being in the Army. In the civilian pictures I've seen of him, he is wearing his hair long. For no reason, really. He just liked long hair, the way he preferred going to parties to being in the Army. The point is, he didn't *represent* anything. He was not a leader or a shirker or a hero. He was just—one of us. And that may be why his death becomes a turning point for us all.

A few hours later, we get the details. Tobi was with a patrol that was opening a section of road. As usual, they were checking both sides of the road for booby traps. After our guys passed, terrorists planted a radio-controlled bomb near the road behind them. When the patrol finished, they climbed onto their trucks for the drive back to base. And that's when it happened. It was a bomb with fifty-five pounds of TNT, and when it went off, it flung the truck to one side of the road, injuring the driver and the squad's tracker. The explosion caught Tobi full in the chest, killing him instantly.

His death is described in the newspaper *Ma'ariv* for June 8, 1987:

Tobi Sadeh Killed in South Lebanon Yesterday, To Be Buried in Haifa Today

. . . The incident happened yesterday at 8:00 A.M. in the T. region in the center of the Security Zone in Southern Lebanon. An IDF patrol in a command car was checking a road. The patrol was on its way back when [the command car] set off a booby trap. Tobi Sadeh was killed on the spot. The driver of the command car and the tracker were injured.

The Islamic Resistance, a military branch of the Hezbollah, boasted in a communique that its "heroic" fighters activated the booby trap.

Lebanese radio reported that in a retaliatory raid by an IDF force and the South Lebanese Army into the village of Shuba, three Shi'ites were killed.

Tobi Sadeh's funeral will take place today at 4:00 P.M. in the military cemetery in Haifa.

The news of Tobi's death disturbed us all, but for Matti and Tommy it was even worse. Matti was on weekend leave when Tobi was killed. He was on his way back to base, hanging around the checkpoint called "The Good Fence," through which Israeli soldiers come and go on their way to duty in Lebanon. The name is a vestige of the '70s, when the Israelis allowed Lebanese wounded in their civil war to be sent to Israeli hospitals. Now, Israel spends three million dollars a year for medical advisers and material to upgrade hospitals in South Lebanon. But patients with serious illnesses, as well as laborers who work in Israel, still pass through that checkpoint, and the old name remains.

Matti was there waiting for a ride from some of the guys in the company when a sergeant who was not even in our unit came up to him and said, "Hey, Matti, sorry about your friend."

"Sorry about what? About who?"

"Didn't you hear? One of the guys in your company was killed this morning."

"Who?" Matti asked. "Who was it?"

"I don't know," said the sergeant. And so for the next couple of hours Matti sat there, waiting, knowing that somebody in his company had been killed but not knowing who it was.

Tommy had a hard time for another reason. On the morning Tobi was killed, Tommy was supposed to have been assigned to clearing that road, but because it was his birthday, he asked Brian, who was in charge of the duty roster, to let him off, and the guy did. So Tommy didn't go out, and Tobi did, and Tobi was killed. Tommy can't get over that and to this day he comes to his birthday with mixed emotions.

It's awful to be at Tobi's funeral. His coffin is wrapped in an Israeli flag and is carried by six guys, Nahal basic trainees, while the rest of us pile into an army truck and follow the procession to the cemetery. There, we stand, lost in a sea of white stones that mark the graves of other men whom you never get to hear about who have been killed in the Army. And all of them so young. Teenagers and adults in their early twenties.

Then there's the whole Jewish idea of the dead. They have to be buried as soon as possible. Even so, because Tobi's death has been reported on the news, everybody knows and the cemetery is full. His parents are there, in shock and weeping. And there is a lot of carrying on by relatives and friends. As things begin to quiet down, the honor guard fires a volley. The sound of shots being fired is not what people need just then, so once more there's an outburst of wailing.

Then, grief or no grief, we have to go back to our base. But that funeral makes a difference to us all. We have crossed some dividing line. We know now that what we have been doing in training is no game. That it's real and that it has consequences. Someone we knew, someone we liked, is gone. Dead.

I corner Sergeant Moshe and insist that he have me transferred back to my unit from the special service I have been doing. Two days later, I get the word, "Pack your stuff. We're coming to get you."

I'm met at the Good Fence by a bunch of our guys, including Mario and Avi, who show up in two APCs. It's a changeover day, a day when one sixth of the unit gets out for a couple of days' leave. The smiles on the guys going home shine through the dust that coats their faces and everything else in sight. For Mario, however, it will prove an exhausting trip. His home is a small kibbutz near Eilat, the southernmost point in Israel. He has a six-hour bus trip each way from the Good Fence to his home and back. He'll just about have time at home for dinner and one night's sleep before he has to start back. Still, he's as cheerful as the other guys. "At least I'll get to sleep in my own bed," he says.

Avi shows me a little black and white puppy that wandered on to the base and that he has adopted. He asks me to feed the pup while he's gone.

"Sure, what does he eat?" I ask.

"Get what you can from the kitchen," he replies.

"How about combat rations?" They certainly taste like dog food to me.

"No. I tried that. He took one sniff and walked away."

We switch places. The dusty guys going home or to be with Tobi's family climb out of the APCs. We clean ones scramble our way into them for the bumpy ride to T. We wind over bare hills which show patches of gray limestone bedrock and through sparse stands of cedar forests. We pass the town of K., then we enter the village of T., where there is a UN checkpoint. After that, we climb a hill past the deserted mansion of an international drug baron.

At the top of the hill, where our base is, we pause. The sky is bright blue, and from here, the view is terrific. On the slopes of the hill are wheat fields interspersed with tiny villages, mere clusters of houses. Opposite us, high on another hill, there stands Beaufort Castle, a Crusader fortress which was used as a strategic point by the PLO until the Golani Brigade Recon Company ousted them in the early days of the 1982 war.

I enter the base, but if I expected a welcoming committee, I'm out of luck. Only a couple of people are around and they're either standing guard or else they're fast asleep. Finally, I go into one of the rooms where I find Matti asleep after being out on patrol for forty hours. I shake him and he opens an eye and kind of smiles as if saying "Nice to see you." He rolls over and mutters, "There's an open bunk over there. See you later." Then he goes back to sleep.

I spend the next little while in the briefing room, where I catch up on what our area is like. Here, in Lebanon, we are issued pocket-sized "Security Guidelines" in which are compressed eight pages of small print intended to clarify our situation for us. The booklet starts with a general explanation of why we are here:

> We are defending the Northern settlements. That is our responsibility and you, as an IDF soldier, are obliged to fulfill this mission with the understanding that the terrorist's path to the center of the country [Israel] cuts through these Northern settlements.

June 1987

Dear Mom and Dad,
I've been in Lebanon since last Thursday. Has it only been three days?

Why did I ask to be sent here? I guess it's partly because my friends are here and partly because one of them, Tobi, was killed by a booby trap. His death trig-

gered off a whole series of events which go a long way
to explaining why we're all up here fighting.

It goes something like this. A kid is suddenly killed
and there's no clear place to lay the blame. Immediately the question that burns hottest is "Why? Why
him? Why now?" And you look for someone to blame.
Fate. Circumstance. God. But that's too abstract. Here,
however, there's a real place to lay the blame. On *them*.
They did it. Hezbollah. PLO. Arabs. They all killed
Tobi. So when we go on an ambush, there's a new
energy for vengeance. If we can hit *them*, great. If not,
you find some other way to express your anger. You're
just not very careful when you're walking through their
gardens. Not so tactful as you search their cars or
houses. What difference does it make? They're all killers. All of them.

And in turn they're probably thinking the same thing
about us. They did it. The Jews who killed three of us
in a retaliatory raid.

So who can blame the Arab kid who's watched us
trample through the family garden or seen his mother
cry as we go through the family house looking for terrorists or been to a funeral for one of his relatives? Is
anyone surprised if he goes out to learn how to ambush
a command car?

We are a group of Israeli soldiers surrounded by an Arab
population. There are Shiite Moslems and Sunni Moslems.
The Shiites are divided into Amal, which just want the Israelis out of Lebanon, and the Hezbollah, who want to kill every
Israeli they can. Then, of course, there are the PLO terrorists, who are divided into half a dozen factions, all of
which bicker and sometimes do battle against each other,
though they are all united in their hatred of us. There are
the Druse and the Christian Arabs, who for the most part,

are friendly to us. The South Lebanese Army, armed and trained by the Israelis, is made up mostly of Christians.

Everyone sees everyone else as a potential enemy. And so, the area is studded with checkpoints at which people are stopped and their papers examined. In the Security Strip alone, there are Israeli Army checkposts, South Lebanese Army checkposts, and UN checkposts. North of the Strip there are a dozen or so armed militias, plus the Syrian Army manning their own checkpoints. One traveler told me he had been stopped eight times between Beirut and Nakura, a small port town near the Israeli border.

The people at all those checkpoints take it as their duty to sort out who has the right to be in any area at any time. This means, for instance, that the twelve-year-old kid I see walking around in civilian clothes who is smoking a cigarette and carrying an AK-47 may be perfectly safe in one zone and will get himself shot in another. Our "Security Guidelines Pamphlet" lists thirty-two suggestions meant to help us decide when to shoot. But at night, things are more straightforward. The order is, "If it moves, shoot it."

Our orders also tell us that there is to be "no contact with the local population." But the local population is there and we can't help seeing them or they us.

Our base is located next to the South Lebanon Army administrative office for the area. This is where the people of the region come when they want to obtain travel papers to Beirut, to get a petition to work in Israel, or to sign up to serve in the SLA. Every morning at seven o'clock all sorts of Lebanese line up on the dusty road outside our main gate. The older Moslems dress traditionally: the men wear dark suits and kefiyahs, the women colorful dresses whose designs vary according to the villages from which they come. The younger Moslems and Christians are more likely to wear

Western-style clothing, although the women prefer to wear dresses rather than pants.

The line quickly gets very long and is controlled by the kind of guy who, in any culture, would be identified as a sleaze. His friends give him the pejorative name "Khomeini" because he is a Shiite. He wears tight tiger-camouflage fatigue pants tucked into his shiny boots. His Kalachnikov AK-47 is slung over his T-shirt, which on any given day has a witty message like, "Well excuse me!" or "Las Vegas Drinking Team." He controls the movement of the line, deciding who gets in first. Sometimes he waves his Kalachnikov threateningly at the crowd if he thinks it is getting disorderly. He drives on and off the base in a small silver BMW, which has a fringe of purple dingleberries hanging in its rear window.

I'm not sure how Khomeini decides just who gets to go first, but as I do guard duty nearby, I can't help noticing that attractive young women and men who take him aside for "a few words" stand a better chance of getting to the head of the line than an elderly Mukhtar, or headman of a nearby village. I'm told, too, that Khomeini is the chief black market operator on the base. For twenty American dollars he can provide a buyer with a quartz Seiko diver's watch, half an ounce of Lebanese blond hash, or a bayonet from an AK-47. A pair of red Israeli paratroop boots, a huge prestige item among the troops in the SLA, can be traded for the entire weapon. So far as I know, no one in my unit has made such a trade.

Tal and I are on guard duty at the main gate. We're listening to 945 AM, WORD, The Voice of Hope Radio. It's a station run by American fundamentalist Christians which plays Jesus rock interspersed with "God's commercials," passages from the Scriptures read in soothing, Southern-accented English. We listen to the station because we can understand what the DJs are saying.

Khomeini, too, is on duty, strutting alongside the line of people waiting to see the civilian administrator. Suddenly an old woman dressed from head to foot in black comes screaming through the gate waving a sickle as she runs. Kicking up dust, she pushes her way through the crowd, shouting hysterically at Khomeini. Khomeini, looking agitated, listens then, leaving her in mid-sentence, turns and bolts into the administration building, from which he returns followed by six SLA soldiers carrying long poles, pikes, and strips of rubber. The woman is still shouting.

I look at Tal. "You don't think they'll hurt her?"

"Nah, she's old . . ."

The voice on Radio Free Lebanon inquires, "Have you evah really looked into yoah soul?"

Khomeini and the soldiers, moving very fast and followed by the old woman, ignore the question as they head for the old woman's field where, we now see, there is smoke rising from a fire. Evidently it was caused by a tracer shell fired by one of our units practicing ambushes nearby. And Khomeini, corrupt enough to trade his rifle for a pair of our boots, is Lebanese enough to drop everything to lead his fellow soldiers on a fire-fighting mission to help the old woman save her field.

Our base is near a regional water distribution plant, where water is collected from the L. River and treated before it is distributed to villages in the area. Once a week an official in a gray suit and white kefiyah shows up at our gate to let the guard know he is coming around to check the gauges and pumps in the control room, which is very near the perimeter of our base. He's careful about letting us know he's coming because an unwarned guard, hearing a suspicious noise one day, took a shot at him. Luckily, the guard was a lousy shot.

Because I hope one day to study fresh water management, I am particularly anxious to meet this expert. When he shows up, an intricate dialogue is set up. The Arab water expert learns third-hand of my interest in his profession. First I explain myself to André, who passes on in French what he has heard to a local schoolteacher, who is waiting for a pass to travel to Beirut. The schoolteacher, in Arabic, tells the water expert that I want to go with him on his tour through the plant. Pleased to be demonstrating his skill to a novice, the water manager leads me into the plant, where in sign language, he explains the uses of his various pipes, gauges, and pumps.

We're returning from a patrol and I'm driving the lead APC. Through the speakers in my headset I can hear Lieutenant Ehud, who is in the command position just behind me. Suddenly, drowning out messages that are coming to us from distant forces using our frequency, I hear Shaltiel, one of the men in the Misfits Platoon, Platoon 1, transmitting orders to Baruch, another Platoon 1 soldier. Shaltiel, with the excitement of a man in the midst of the biggest engagement in years, calls, "Two, this is Ringo. Take us through the fire. That's right. Give me some 81-millimeter mortar. Good shooting. Two, call for artillery; we're going in. Artillery. This is Ringo. Give me cover at coordinates . . ."

What's happened is clear to me. Shaltiel and Baruch, who are playing out the moves in an imaginary war, are in an APC parked at their post and are not aware that the broadcast switch of their radio is on and that the entire region is listening to the progress of their "war." "Two," calls Shaltiel, "get me helicopters. I need more support . . ."

Lieutenant Ehud, using the code name Shaltiel has given his imaginary unit, tries to break in: "Ringo, Ringo, this is Watermelon. Call a cease-fire. Cease-fire. Over."

Shaltiel is oblivious. He either doesn't hear Ehud or else

he is too caught up in his command responsibilities to pay
attention to the entreaties of a mere lieutenant. Ehud tries a
couple of times again, "Ringo, Ringo . . ." but the war just
rages on. Finally, as Shaltiel is calling for a full air strike,
Ehud, abandoning any attempt at civility or radio code
bursts out, "Dammit to hell, Shaltiel. This is Ehud. If you
don't get off this band right away, I'm going to come over
and kick your ass myself. Understood?"

Silence.

Then, hesitantly, "All forces, this is Ringo. Cease-fire.
Cease-fire. Over and out."

In the folk wisdom of the Israeli Army, soldiers are divided
into two sorts: *Rosh Gadol* and *Rosh Katan,* big heads and
little heads. A little head does what he is told and doesn't do
it until he is told to. Once at work, he does only what is
necessary to get by. A big head is someone who knows what
has to be done without having to be told and does it as well
as it can possibly be done. Here, in Lebanon, much to my
surprise, most of us have become "big heads." Because we
are in real danger, we take our two hours a day of guard duty
very seriously. Though our sergeants and officers no longer
hound us for every little infraction, we find ourselves taking
special care of our equipment. Even though we are in dry
country where we could probably get away without cleaning
our guns every single night, we clean them anyway. Nobody
needs to remind us that if our guns aren't clean enough, they
may jam. And a jammed gun can get you killed.

Along with the constant blocks of guard duty, most of our
time is spent clearing the roads or setting ambushes. We go
out every day divided into two columns, one on each side of
the road. Usually, we follow a Bedouin tracker as we ex-
amine the road for booby traps. But the most demanding
work we do is setting ambushes of our own.

An ambush takes very careful planning, sometimes as

much as twelve hours, because everyone has to be thoroughly briefed on every aspect of our position. And we talk through every possibility: what to do if we're attacked from such and such an angle; what to do if the patrol leader is hurt or killed; who will take command; how to get back to the base. Every member of the patrol has to know how to operate whatever equipment we're carrying. Every man must know how to operate the radio so that, if necessary, he can call in helicopter or artillery support. We do a mock ambush next to our base, where we practice all the possibilities we have discussed, then after a final briefing, we set out, usually before dusk, for a spot that our intelligence people have reason to believe infiltrators are likely to pass. Sometimes all they have to go on are educated guesses: certain villages are hotbeds of Hezbollah or PLO activity; and some routes, because of the nature of the terrain, are the ones likely to be used. Our task is to set our ambush at some strategic point on that route.

As we move, we are constantly on the lookout. Sometimes we follow behind a tank riding in APCs. The tank has enormous rollers in front of its own treads that are designed to trigger a mine without endangering the tank crew. Unfortunately, the rollers are spaced for Centurion M-60A1 tanks treads and *not* for the APC M-113 Zelda armored personnel carrier in which we are riding. The APC driver can only be sure that *one* of his treads is not going to go up on a mine. And if the APC does, forget it—they aren't designed to withstand that sort of explosion. So it's pretty harrowing driving an APC to an ambush site.

The work is harrowing, too, because the intelligence reports are not always accurate. While we are on our way to set an ambush, the enemy may already be in place somewhere along our route, ready to ambush us. In fact, that's how a group of Givati soldiers were killed in this region a few months ago. Ambushed on their way to set an ambush.

It sounds grim and mostly it is. But not always. On one of my first ambushes I'm lying next to Lieutenant Ehud. It's a starlit night. I'm wide awake. Suddenly both Ehud and I tense as we hear a noise in the bushes off to the right. I grab my Galil and hold it tight. All my senses are wired. Ehud whispers, "I'll be right back," and crawls away into the night, leaving me his night scope.

"What the—shit." I've never felt so alone. I've got five guys behind me but it's me with the radio, me with the night scope, me that will have to lead a charge now that Ehud's gone.

I look for him through the night scope and see his green shape against the green starlit sky. He's scuffling with something in the bushes. I slip the safety catch from my rifle and twist myself around so I can sight in on Ehud and his antagonist, but he has disappeared from view. A minute later he's back. "Here," he says, tossing me a small furry ball. "Here's our infiltrator." The ball unwinds itself, becomes a hedgehog, and scampers away.

"What's the matter, Wolf," Ehud says as I give him back his scope. "Your hand's shaking."

"Yeah," I reply. "Chilly night."

I'm exhausted, too tired to sleep. I've been up for forty-two hours.

Up at 3:30 A.M. for guard duty. From 4:30 to 5:15 A.M., dawn alert. We all go to our stations around the base. At 5:30, eat. Eggs, bread, jam, salad, and coffee. Prepare the armored personnel carrier. Its metal is cold, but it heats up quickly, like the day. Then we go off to open the roads.

It is a bright, clear, warm morning but there is dust everywhere from the movement of our equipment. The roads down which we wind are in bad shape because so much

heavy traffic has gone over them. We pass through the village of T., where all life seems to have come to a stop. The
children make hesitant attempts to wave at us, but the adults
simply watch us blankly. A shepherd hurries his flock to the
side of the road. His sheep bleat and push each other in
their haste to get out of the way of the armored personnel
carrier. The air is filled with the smells of gasoline, sheep,
and Arab cooking.

Our guys walk on both sides of the road checking for
wires, barrels, anything that looks suspicious. The armored
personnel carriers rumble behind us. When we get to clumps
of trees, the machine gunner shoots bursts of "preventive
fire."

As radio carrier for Ehud, I walk immediately behind
him. Though the radio pack I carry is heavier than other
pakalim, it's easier to carry because I get to walk in the
middle of the road while the guys searching the sides are
stumbling over rocks and tripping over branches. When we
reach the end of our assigned section of road, we pile onto
the armored personnel carriers and are driven back to the
base, where almost immediately we are assigned to escort
military staff officers through the area.

At four o'clock, we are sent to prepare another ambush.
But first dinner. Again, eggs, bread, jam, salad, coffee. Then
we're off. On our way we blow up a Katyusha rocket that is
found pointing at the Hula Valley in Israel.

Dusk. After an hour's walk, we set up the ambush.

Midnight. Bright stars overhead. I'm lying on my stomach, cradling my Galil assault rifle. I can hear the guys
breathing on either side of me. From the pace of the breathing I can tell who's asleep and who's awake. Every so often,
I hear the rustling of paper as someone unwraps a snack and
the crunch as it is eaten. . . .

As spring advances, we go on one nerve-racking patrol after another. At night, in the high hills where we are, it can still be very cold, but now, midafternoons warm up. As it gets closer to spring, we find ourselves setting up our ambushes in balmy weather under clear skies. There is a strange beauty in moving out to set an ambush just at dusk. We are in olive green fatigue uniforms as we wade through the golden wheat fields in night formation. The wheat bends under us as we flow over the terraces; fireflies flash around us as we weave our way through blossoming orchards. And silence.

I remember swimming through phosphorous flashes on a night scuba dive in the sea off Carmel. There was the same fluid motion. The same darkness. The same flashes of light and the same stillness. Is it any less beautiful this time because we may have to kill people?

Usually we spend nights at our ambush sites alternately watching for the enemy and following the moon and the stars moving through their courses. One of the ways to stay awake is to watch Orion rise and do a half twist around the North Star.

From our vantage point we can see Arab villages to the north and west, and Israeli border villages to the east. As we lie there, armed, wearing helmets and flak jackets, I feel no ambiguities about why I am here. Yesterday patrols like ours intercepted and hit three separate groups of terrorists trying to cross into Israel. The issue is very clear. "They" want to cross the line to hurt us, and "we" are here to stop them.

One night, my squad follows a tank. I'm invited inside the tank, which is equipped with a night vision device. The commander is watching a screen on which the terrain in front of us is displayed schematically. It's like being inside a video arcade. Because the night vision device senses heat differences, we can actually see people moving as stick figures across the terrain. They appear on the screen in dark black.

My first day: a real *bizzbuzz*.

In the field.

Finally, a cohesive unit.

Building a temporary base "somewhere in the north."

A view from our base in Lebanon.

Paratroop training to get our wings.

Ninety kilometers to Jerusalem...

...and the red beret.

The "uprising." Action... Zoom 77/Gamma-Liaison

...and reaction. Chip Hires/Gamma-Liaison

And because it is night, and because they are in a zone
where they have no business being, and because our intelligence has warned us of enemy action in this area, our tank
fires a series of rounds.

Each antipersonnel shell the tank fires has twelve thousand tiny metal arrows. The figures on our screen are more
than a half a mile away. What happens on the screen is a
tiny silent movie. As our shells explode, we see the stick
figures on the screen changing color as they lose heat, as
they lose life. Figures that were dark black now turn a
lighter and lighter color. They become various shades of
gray until finally they appear on our screen as white shapes,
which means they are cold.

That, then, is my first encounter with the enemy. There
are no screams. There are no bodies to look at. There is only
this silent transition from warmth to cold, from black to
white on a TV screen. What we know is that there were
people on their way to harm us, and now there aren't. That's
it.

Another night, another ambush.

We lie still and wait for the time to pass. Sometime in the
course of our waiting, a third of the squad gets a break and
we wriggle back to the APC for a hot drink from our thermoses or a light snack. A few of us at a time are allowed to
sleep. There's nothing fancy about the nap. We put our
heads down on our helmets and are asleep. The guys who
have to stay awake have worked out some tricks. One of
them is to put their helmets underneath their chests. That
way, if their heads start to loll forward, they get a sharp pain
that starts them awake.

But the real thing that keeps you awake when you have to
be is that if you fall asleep you could get killed. Over and
over, we repeat to ourselves the warning, "Routine kills."
You've got to be alert; you can't let routine interfere with

your reaction time because delay of even a second or two can turn out to be deadly. Or we rehearse dangerous scenarios in our heads as we wait. That rock out there—there may be someone hiding behind it. Any minute now, he's going to jump out at me. Or looking at a nearby hill, you think, "That's a good hiding place for a group of terrorists."

What it amounts to is this: you constantly have a clear vision of your own death. You see the gleam of the mine, you hear its explosion. It's as if the whole world around you is an inflated balloon and there you are poking at it with a pin. You're just waiting for it to pop.

Eventually, it does. In my case, my unit never came under fire while we were in ambush, but we did attack from an ambush position and you could feel the tension of waiting dissipate the minute the firing began. From that moment on you concentrate and do what needs to be done. It's only the long waiting that is scary.

And it's always with you here. Your head is on a swivel all the time. All directions are dangerous, as is every action of every day and night. On guard, on patrol, in an ambush. And even when you're not directly on duty, you don't stop being alert. Eating or sleeping or taking a crap, your gun is next to you, the magazine is in, there's a shell in the chamber.

You sense how awful that tension is when for a while it is no longer with you. When, for instance, I go home to the kibbutz and go through the gates, I feel the tension lifting. The constant prickle at the back of my neck disappears and I feel as if I'm about to have a warm bath or a massage, or climb into a soft bed.

Tonight, I'm not on the kibbutz. I'm here. Tired, but straining to keep alert because an intelligence report has reached us that we're likely to be attacked. By 4 A.M. it's clear that the intelligence report is wrong. We fold up the ambush and open the road back to the base.

On our way we move in two columns, checking both sides of the road. In a choreographed exchange of territory, we soldiers head toward home while the local fieldworkers, mostly women wearing the traditional dresses of their villages, take our places on the road and in the fields. In one hand, the women carry their food in cloth sacks—pita, olives, and cucumbers—in the other, the sharpened scythes or sickles with which they will harvest their wheat.

The women are usually escorted by an older man astride a donkey who, though he wears a kefiyah to ward off the sun, wears black pants and a black suit jacket over his white cotton shirt. Though some of the women in his group are older than he is, none of them gets to ride.

Sometimes we stop such a group for searches. What gets to me is how patient they are as we make them open their food sacks and sniff at their water bottles. They look at us ironically, as if to say, "Yes, we've seen armies like you before. You come and go, but we'll always be here to harvest the wheat, season after season."

Mostly, the villagers are patient, but today one of them is not. As we are clearing the roads, we find a suspicious wire sticking out of the embankment on one side of the road. We immediately stop all road traffic while we investigate. The Lebanese driver of a Volkswagen van, which is the lead vehicle on the road, becomes increasingly exasperated with every passing minute. His van is piled high with crates of chickens. "My chickens will die in the heat," he complains. But we can't permit the traffic to move until the sappers have examined the wire. So the traffic does not move.

The irritated driver gets out of his van, kicks his tires, drums on the door. As the heat of the sun intensifies, so does the squawking of the unhappy chickens. He looks at us, looks at the wire, looks at the chickens. Finally, he can stand it no longer. He strides up to the troublemaking wire and grabs it with both hands. All of us, soldiers and civilians, stiffen with alarm as we wait for the blast we think will come. André, the sniper, who is standing behind me, drops to the ground.

There is a "poof" as the wire comes free, and the now triumphant, but still angry, van driver flings it to one side. Even with my shaky Arabic I understand the gist of what he says as he climbs back into his van: "Idiots! A simple wire. *Now* can I go?"

I give Lieutenant Ehud the handset so he can call off the sappers. I don't know if you can tell relief on a chicken's face, but these chickens look relieved.

June 21, 1987

Yesterday morning, after opening the road, we got word that one of our patrols ran head-on into a group of five terrorists who were armed to the teeth: boxes of TNT, grenades, Kalachnikovs. They're from a village close by which, because it is a Hezbollah garrison, has been a target for several of our ambushes. Anyway, our guys hit them. This time the action was close up and not the video game hit of a tank ambush. Our soldiers moved into action just as they were taught in basic training. Three of the enemy were killed on the spot, but the other two took off into a nearby wooded wadi. As he ran, one of them threw a grenade at my friend David. The grenade landed about twenty-five feet from him and exploded, but David was unhurt.

I was with a group higher up, opening the roads. We rushed to the western edge of the wadi to close it off. From our vantage point, I watched as two Hughes Defender helicopters joined in the search for the two terrorists. Meanwhile, our guys in the wadi were being shelled by artillery from the village. A barrage from our own artillery silenced those guns.

The grenade thrower disappeared into the woods and we never did find him. The fifth man was spotted by one of our tanks. The tank gunner fired one round that started a small fire but missed the man. The second round he fired was a concussion shell, designed to stop a tank or a whole platoon of soldiers. When it went off, the terrorist just disappeared.

How to explain the jubilation here over the engagement? Why are the people who weren't down in the wadi where the action was jealous? The brigade commander sent us a bottle of champagne and we toasted the guys who were in the fight.

The patrol that killed those men was out for twelve hours and came back exhilarated, heading straight for the kitchen. I cornered Alan, the Chicagoan whose specialty is falling in love and who was one of the men on that patrol. "Hey, Alan," I said. "Tell me something. You've been trained as a medic. You've had a three-month course learning how to save lives. How do you feel now that you've killed some-body."

"How do I feel?" he said. "I feel hungry."

That brief battle, the first one in which we were personally and directly engaged, answers a couple of questions for all of us, even those who weren't on the wadi floor. "Will I be able to pull the trigger in combat?" "Will I stay calm?" The answer each time is "yes."

That night, when I stand guard, I briefly entertain the idea of killing a stray cat that is making a racket. And then I realize I can't. More than that, I understand that I probably will never go hunting.

Dear Mom and Dad,
It's so hard to have a hundred letters inside of you and not be able to do anything with them. I guess the only solution is this—write down as often as I can what's happening and then send you the whole thing when I'm out of here—then you won't have to worry so much.

June 23

The routine is starting to make sense. What bothers me is that I'm getting used to it.

I think I'm changing and in a way that I don't like. In the beginning, in pre-basic, one of the Hebrew teachers asked what we were afraid of. Aside from the usual fears of death and maiming, one person (maybe it was me) said he was scared he would become harder. Well, I think it's happening. When you see enough that screams against both logic and morals at the same time as you confront the fact that you can kill and do it easily, there is a certain protective reflex—you start to take stuff lightly—if only to stay sane. So you affect cynicism to an exaggerated degree and you let yourself push what you thought of as important values to one side: thoughtfulness, compassion, liberality.

Last night we were moved out to a village where one of our "security people" (informer in English) was shot at. We simply closed the town, rounded up the men, and had them questioned by Intelligence.

June 24

I'm out on leave!

I was driven to a base overlooking the Hula Valley. The minute we crossed the border and I dusted myself off, I swear I could smell civilian life. It took dropping my guard for me to realize how tense I've been. It's like the times when I went home to my kibbutz—the minute I entered its gates I could feel the relief.

Nice feeling, freedom.

June 26

Oh, beautiful, beautiful civilian life. Hung out on my kibbutz, then went to Tel Aviv with Jake, basking in normalcy.

June 28

Back on the base.

We had a quiet ambush last night. Everyone's nervous for two reasons:

1. We've less than two weeks of duty left here. A time when our guard naturally drops. We have to be careful of getting sloppy.

2. Since we hit the terrorists, they've made no further move. No mines, no attacks. Word has it that they're planning something big. But what does word know? In any case, we're doing our best to stay alert. Doubling our patrols, changing our routines.

Should be a hot night.

I love you.

July 2

Well, it turned out relatively quiet. We were the support force for our reconnaisance company on an operation over the S. River. The company was to cross over to mine an old IDF stronghold that has been taken over by terrorists. We were divided into two forces on this side of the S. If the group that crossed over should need help (there was an 80 percent chance of engagement), the rest of us would go over with a tank, two APCs, a doctor, and an ambulance. There was still another support group that included attack helicopters, artillery, and a certain number of paratroopers with night vision devices.

The fortress lay between two villages, F. and A. As our recon company reached the last house in F., it was hit by an ambush. One of the guys was lightly wounded in the hand. Then for the next two hours we covered their retreat with tank shells and artillery—killing at least two terrorists and destroying six houses.

Amazing how highly organized an army operation is. I have a scary thought: Maybe one of the reasons we are still in Lebanon is the invaluable training we get. The idea is scary, but not so far-fetched.

An aside: Driving an APC in Lebanon is a very satisfying experience for anyone who has ever been stuck in rush-hour traffic. In an APC you can literally drive right over anything that gets in your way, which may be why nothing ever does. Anyone who sees us coming pulls over to the side. Everyone, that is, except the UN vehicles.

We never make aggressive gestures against the UN. Their patrols are carefully scheduled. We are advised when they are coming and they take care to make themselves very visible. They drive white jeeps with the letters UN written all over them. In addition to that, they fly the United Nations flag, on which they train spotlights so everyone for miles around can see it.

July 5

Well, the Fourth of July almost slipped by before I even noticed it. I've been here too long.

We had a great barbecue yesterday. Sergeant Moshe really has come into his own since we got here. He collected money from the officers to start a company PX, then with the profits he made selling us Cokes, cigarettes, and chips, he's been renting video tapes for us to see. And yesterday, for the second time, he showed up with pitas, humous, salad fixings, and strips of meat and chicken.

I was well into my third chicken-and-humous sandwich when I remembered that it was the Fourth of July. When I asked Alan and David and some of the other Americans if they remembered what day it was, they didn't know what I was talking about.

You remember Brian, the Englishman who fantasizes himself as Ironman? He's become the company's record keeper. He juggles guard duty lists and patrol rosters with a precision and fairness that is a wonder to us all. He can remember not only how many hours and minutes each of us has stood guard but also the exact weight of the load each guy carried on a patrol, and he shifts our duty assignments so skillfully that not a man in the company complains.

The guy who has changed most in our group is Nathan, who called you from Washington when he was on leave. Ever since he got over his hesitation with the Galil, he's been more and more comfortable with his own weapons and with those used by the platoon. He's been made a MAGist. The same guy who had to be coaxed to pull off a single shot in basic now lets loose with long bursts of "preventive fire," every morning on patrol.

Hard as it is here, both physically and emotionally, I'm going to be sorry when we go back to training. At least here the work has a very real point, and when we've finished our training, our assignments most likely will be on the West Bank or Gaza. There, the thrust of the work is against the civilian population. Here it's against real terrorists and our contact with civilians is incidental.

One of the guys in the platoon says our training is meant to make us reflexive killers. Automatons, without a will of our own. Someone else says, "Yes, we're trained to act automatically, but each of us is responsible for drawing our own moral line of behavior which we will not cross."

They may both be right. Here are some recent examples.

On one occasion, we were passing through a village,

and out of the corner of my eye, I saw a pistol being pointed at me. It was as if I was looking through a zoom lens that had focused only on a gun. My own gun was set for automatic fire; my finger was on the trigger. I was about to let loose a burst of fire when some part of me registered that the blurry image behind the gun pointed at me was only four feet tall. So I didn't pull the trigger, though according to my training, I should have. And if I had, I would have killed a kid holding a plastic gun. On the other hand, even kids have shot real guns at our guys.

There was also the time when we were driving along the coast and I heard a huge explosion to my right. There, standing in the water, was a man getting ready to throw what looked like a grenade at us. The driver slammed on the brakes, and I grabbed up my gun and got the guy in my sights when it occurred to me to wonder why he was wearing a bathing suit. And so I didn't shoot some poor fisherman who had been dynamite fishing in the ocean.

But I must confess that the trained soldier in me, acting reflexively, has made me come very close to killing several bushes and rocks which, I swear, moved threateningly toward me.

I don't know what all this says about the human condition or conditioning. I'll sort it out later.

July 6, 5:25 A.M.
One of our tanks just went up on a mine. The explosion makes a sick BOOM. Then there is gunfire. One tank crew member is lightly wounded. The exhilaration of action turns flat when our guys are in danger.

Two more days. Then we're out of Lebanon.

July 7
Laid a quiet ambush last night. Pretty. After the moon

set, the stars really burned. Bizarrely beautiful to lie there on an isolated hillside on a soft summer night.

Tomorrow we're out of here.

Finally, what is there to say? I'm glad I pushed to come here. I'm glad I saw it. On the other hand, I think of the deaths, theirs and ours, and I wonder.

Anyhow, thanks for helping me through this. As I wrote, I kept thinking of sitting in our living room and telling you about it. It was good to think that. I know some parts aren't clear. Remember, I was usually exhausted while writing. I'm sure you understand why I couldn't mail all this until I was out.

I love you,

A.

P.S. I know you never believed my story that I was in Eilat guarding the beaches against submarine attacks, but thanks for not letting on.

9

We're out of Lebanon. We pack up our gear, brief the paratroop recon company that replaces us at our base, and start to roll east—toward the Good Fence and Israel. Khomeini waves goodbye as we leave. I think he's happy to see us go. We were lousy customers.

As we get to the border, Ehud sets off a smoke grenade. A green plume rises from his APC. Then Eli fires off a gray one. Suddenly the rest of us are scrambling for spares and setting them off. Pow. Green, gray, blue, red smoke wafts upward on all sides. We are leaving Lebanon.

Avi's worried about his puppy. Because of shady characters like Khomeini, the MPs search troops coming in from Lebanon looking for contraband: hash, watches, alcohol. Avi thinks his dog may be considered contraband. We don't take any chances and hide the dog in André's sniper pack.

At the Good Fence we have a few minutes for a felafel and a cup of coffee at a food stand run by Hannah, a middle-aged Yemenite woman and her exquisitely beautiful nineteen-year-old daughter. Hannah knows most of us soldiers be-

178

cause we have spent long hours at the Good Fence waiting for transport or beginning and ending escort duty. The food stand's customers are usually soldiers and tourists who have come to marvel at the way the Good Fence works. Hannah is partial to the soldiers, to whom she serves free coffee. We, for our part, are always grateful for the coffee and pleased at the sight of her daughter.

Today Hannah gives us more than coffee. She has baked a lemon cake topped with white frosting on which, in blue letters, she has written, *kol hakavod.* "All honor to you." It's good to be home.

The celebratory mood persists back in Israel, where we hear *kol hakavod* frequently reiterated. For a week while we sign off on our equipment and prepare the new temporary base for the next section of the battalion, we go from party to party. A company party, a battalion party. We eat a great deal of roast chicken. We watch skits in which officers mimic enlisted men and vice versa. We hear speeches and watch slide shows that praise our year of working together. We attend a concert that bills Yoram Gaon and the popular Nahal Band, in which such famous performers as Arik Einstein and Gaon, himself, got their start; we sing along with songs such as "Aman Aman" and "When I Was a Civilian." The mood is continuously upbeat. All the skits and songs are cheery, either satirizing some aspect of army life or expressing our longing to be civilians again. There are no dirty words in any of the songs we sing. Even the slang expression "a broken prick," which is usually used to indicate ultimate despair, is transformed in the songs to "a broken tail."

Finally, we say our goodbyes. Company Aleph has been together for a long, difficult year. Not everyone has made it. And now, because length of service is based on a variety of factors—age, marital status—most of the immigrants, who are older, are being discharged. The younger sabras, who all serve three years, are going to their *He' Achzut*, their six-month period of agricultural training on a border outpost.

Six of us immigrants are bound for the 50th Nahal Battalion of the Paratroop Brigade. Besides myself, there are Danno from Australia; Manni, the Argentine ex-pilot; David, the MAGist from New Jersey; Tommy the Mancunian; and Mario from Milan.

Back on the kibbutz for a week's leave, I am struck by the contrast between the way Israeli soldiers are treated by the civilian populace and the way some Americans have treated their own veterans. And it isn't because everyone in Israel supports the government in its policies on the West Bank or in Lebanon. Plenty of people, including some of the soldiers themselves, have their doubts about the morality of our presence there. But the doubts—even the anger—are never expressed as mistreatment of the guys who have to be there. Everyone knows that being a soldier is tough, and even people who disagree with the government's policies have no trouble at all sending Care packages to soldiers who, after all, are their sons or brothers or fathers.

All through my army service, I've felt the support of the people around me. Friends have given me the keys to their apartments "just in case you have a free couple of hours and need a shower." Or they have put me up for a week at a time when I had to be near an army hospital far from my kibbutz. Most merchants and movie theaters offer discounts to soldiers. Drivers who have picked me up hitchhiking have gone miles out of their way to make sure that I got home in time for the Sabbath. Once on a routine patrol at Shmurat Dan, a popular picnic area, Manni and I, in full gear and detailed to look for suspicious objects, had our work continually interrupted by picknickers calling, "Hey, soldiers. Come and have some chicken." "Hey, come on over for some steak." "Thirsty? How about a Coke?"

Back on the kibbutz, my welcome is especially warm. Everyone knows where I've been and I get smiles and pats on the back and more friendly *"kol hakavods."* Because like everyone else in the country each of them has been in a similar situation. Each of them understands.

The 50th Battalion has a permanent base in the middle of the country, but we're told we won't be seeing much of it. Our schedule for the next six months starts, as every new training period does, with an intense two week *gibbush*—this time in the Judean Desert. After that, we'll move on to an air force base, where our paratroop training will begin. Once we get our wings and do a march to Jerusalem for our red beret, we'll do a squad leader's course and more large-scale maneuvers. After which we're scheduled for three weeks of "border patrol," probably somewhere on the West Bank.

The mood in the new base is different from the one I'm used to. For one thing, we are now a small group of immigrants in a sabra platoon, which in turn, is part of a sabra company. The sabras are puzzled by our presence. "You mean you could be in America right now, driving a Cadillac and living with movie stars, and instead you're here running around in the desert? Man, you're crazy. You don't even need a green card."

For all their talk about Cadillacs and movie stars, the guys on this base who have been in the army for eighteen months have the look and feel of veterans and it's clear to me that they won't give us the kinds of problems we had with the "Nightmare Garin." Because they *have* been around for a while, they have a sense not only of what needs to be done, but also of what they can get away with. As we sign on new equipment, there isn't one guy who doesn't argue with the supply personnel to get the best gear available.

But these guys are not goof-offs. They have chosen to be here. Shachar, of Romanian descent, who has been carrying a MAG for a year and a half, is a tall thin guy with a patchy beard, who has a passion for the singer Yehudit Ravitz. Shachar is subject to asthma attacks and like Gil, a medic from the same *garin* who has bad knees, and Boaz, a burly, balding only son of an Iraqi family, he could have avoided being in a combat unit. When he is asked why he chose paratroop training he replies, "Where else could I go? The 'Eight Zero Five' battalion?"

When I don't understand the reference, Gil explains that the "Eight Zero Five" is a mythical unit where "You show up at eight, do zero work, and go home at five."

Though Ehud, Eli, and Moshe, our officers in basic, drove us hard, I find myself feeling nostalgia for them when I compare them to the men who are in charge of us now. Lieutenant Shuki, our new company commander, is of Moroccan descent. He is a dark man with bushy eyebrows that arch menacingly over his eyes. Watching those eyes, I understand the Israeli expression for a certain kind of two-faced person: *Ayin tzochecet ve'ayin dofeket.* "One eye laughs with you while you get fucked by the other." As Shuki switches between jokes and threats, his eyes alternately glint and glower.

Ari, our platoon commander, is a native kibbutznik with blue eyes and straight blond hair. Though he seems friendly as he gives the orders to get our new *pakalim* in order, he seems not to care very much about the problems that crop up: no batteries in our field radios, no chin straps for our helmets, no sniper for our platoon. When these matters are brought to his attention, he says absently, *"Yihyeh beseder.* It'll be OK."

Our NCOs aren't much more reassuring. Benny, our tall, lanky staff sergeant is due to be discharged from the army soon and he seems more concerned with checking off the remaining days on his calendar than with anything that might promote our welfare. Yokhai, an enormous sergeant who, except for his blond hair, is the spit and image of Li'l

Abner, means to do right by us, but he hasn't been in the Army any longer than we have, so nothing he says carries the weight of authority.

But if these guys don't glitter with leadership, we comfort ourselves with the frequently repeated Israeli phrase of consolation: *Ze ma she'yesh, ve im zeh nenatzeach.* "That's what there is and with it we will be victorious." So what if we are led by men I would hesitate to follow to the firing range, let alone into the desert for advanced training; and what if we have no chin straps or batteries, or a sniper for our platoon? It's what we have, and with it, we begin our *gibbush.*

If I had problems with the cold in Lebanon, the heat in the Judean Desert creates problems of its own.

It's really hot. The temperature can hit 120 degrees, 110 in the shade. I've been cold and I've been hot. I prefer cold anytime. With cold, as it was in the Golan Heights, you could get away from it once in a while. You might escape it in your sleeping bag for a few minutes, before the rain finally soaked through, but you can't do that with heat. There's nowhere to go. The heat is there, every minute. It's hot when you're guarding, when you're walking, when you're running. It's more insidious than rain. It's heavier than any burden I have ever carried. It's hot.

You drink all the time because there's the constant threat of dehydration, but there's no way to drink yourself cool. I drink off one canteen and, boom, I'm on the second. I feel the water dissipating even as it goes down my throat. Dissipating so it never seems to reach my stomach. It goes out through my pores, evaporating so quickly it creates a new form of torment. I get a salt crust on my fatigues that immediately sets my skin to itching and keeps the air from circulating through my clothes.

The idea of this *gibbush*, too, is that if you push the men, they have to count on each other for help and that will create tight working relationships. So in that heat, they push us.

For two weeks straight. Always on the move, always marching, always running. If you get to sleep for an hour and a half, you're lucky.

The loose, black basalt of the Golan made for difficult walking and dangerous running. Here, in the desert, we deal with white rock: limestone, chalk, chert. You see the strata formed by the skeletons of creatures that lived in ancient seas. But the strata, rather than lying horizontally, twist and fold from the tremendous pressures of the nearby Syrio-African rift. Strange designs are formed by the meandering lines of age-old goat paths. In biblical times, this area was green and lush and supported herds of goats and sheep. The young David found a good spot here where he could hide from Saul's wrath. Now, after two thousand years of over-grazing, the region is a desert in which, as part of our training, we are taught to mount assaults against troops made of green cardboard.

At night, our boots set off sparks when they strike the rocks. And wherever we go, day or night, we stir up white chalk dust as we walk, making soft clouds with every step. We breathe the dust. It gets into our lungs, our clothes. From the knees down, we are white with dust. From the waist up, we are white from the encrusted salt of our sweat. Despite our sunburnt skins, we look ghostly and drawn.

Sometime in the middle of the second week, our platoon is assigned the task of taking a very steep hill in mock battle. To get to it, we have to march six miles, timing ourselves to arrive at dawn. The idea is that we're supposed to take the hill before the sun actually rises. We take the hill, but by the time its ours, the sun is high in the sky. Lieutenant Shuki thinks we moved too slowly so the command comes, "Do it again." So down we come and up we charge, conquering it again. A mile and a half straight up. We're finally at the top, exhausted. "Still too slow, take that hill again." And down we go for the third time. The sun is now broiling. We sweat, we drink, we climb down. We sweat, we drink, we climb up and conquer the damn hill for the third time. "Better," Shuki says. "Not good, but better."

Now we have to march six miles back to the base. It is these last six miles that finally wipe us out. On the way down the path, three guys fall over, dehydrated. Four more drop on the way back to the base. Those of us still marching look on enviously as the guys who collapsed are driven back to the base in the trucks we called in.

I just make it back to base, but I am so weak that all I can do is crawl into my tent, where I collapse. I lie there, listless and dizzy and hot. And then comes the diarrhea, the kind that makes you think, "Oh my God, I have to go to the bathroom," at almost the same time as you think, "Oh my God, I just went to the bathroom." It's all terribly degrading —but I'm just too tired to care. The diarrhea is dangerous, too, because with it you lose even more body fluids.

Luckily for me, one of the platoon medics comes by and sees me lying there looking like hell. He puts a hand to my forehead and says, "Dehydration. Man, you're going to the clinic."

So I spend a day and a half in the hospital getting a total of five infusions and having cold compresses packed around me. Well, it's one way to beat the heat.

Advanced infantry training may be advanced, but when you come right down to it, it's a real pain in the ass. We've done most of this stuff before, only now we're doing it longer and harder. After serving in Lebanon, where everything we did was important, all this running and shooting seems pointless.

And the pointlessness, plus our fatigue, intensifies the ambivalence we feel about our officers and NCOs and, finally, about the training itself. There is a sharp drop in our morale. We stop giving our all during exercises. Guys refuse to wake up for guard duty. Boaz, attaching himself to a passing group of tourists, goes AWOL.

I overhear a couple of guys standing guard in a nearby platoon: "So the thing to do is complain about knee or back problems. They can't tell if it's real so they *have* to lay you up for a couple of days at least."

"But if you really need the break," the second guy says, "here's what you do. You catch two bees and put each one in a drinking glass. Then you press the mouth of each glass to either side of your knee. When the bees get angry enough, they'll sting you. You take that swollen knee to the doctor and you've got yourself a week off at least."

"Bees," says the first guy. "Wow. Bees."

The pressures of life on this base are getting to all of us; relations between noncombat and combat soldiers are strained. In theory, there ought to be no problem. We are, after all, on the same side and we have to rely on each other. Without the supply soldiers and cooks, the combat units would bog down. And in wartime we are even more interdependent. There are plenty of times when soldiers from Communications or other support units are right up on the front lines with the ground forces. Truck drivers risk their lives to bring food or warm clothing to the guys at the front.

Still, problems can develop. For obvious reasons, combat training has some prestige attached to it. And some guy who, because he has bad knees or flat feet, has to spend his service counting boots or cutting onions has no trouble nursing a certain amount of resentment against the combat guys, who get all the glory.

At the same time, a combat soldier who has spent the day running up and down hills busting his butt can get mighty resentful of a guy working an eight-hour day in a real build-

ing—not a tent—who has access to hot coffee, TV, VCRs.
And women. They're around women every single day!

For the second time, I'm spending a birthday in the Army.
My platoon is assigned kitchen duty in the base dining room.
Tommy, Danno, and I are clearing the dinner tables when we
run into a problem. There is trouble with the pipes, and most
of the base, except for the kitchen, is out of hot water—
including the outdoor dishwashing area. How are we going
to get our dishes washed?

The simplest solution is to go into the kitchen and do our
dishes in its two monster sinks. The trouble is that the army
cook in charge has no interest in simple solutions.

The cook, a tall, dark, curly-headed guy is at a table slicing carrots. I tell him I'm from Company Aleph, and I ask
him if we can use his sinks to wash our company's dishes.

He hears me but there are ten more slices of carrots before he replies. "No." In the interval, other kitchen workers
drift up and take positions behind the carrot slicer.

"What do you mean, no?" Tommy is at my right, Manny
at my left. Mario and Danno are right behind them.

"It's what I mean. No." Carrot slices proliferate. My guys
fidget. His guys fidget.

"Come on," I say. "We're in the same army. We're on the
same side."

"No."

"OK," I say. "Forget patriotism. Forget army spirit. Do it
for me. A personal favor." There is laughter on both sides of
the line.

The guy slicing carrots is implacable. "No."

I try being Machiavellian. "Look," I say. "Company
Aleph has a problem and you're the only one who can solve
it. What do you say?"

"No." I hear Mario muttering under his breath.

"Look, I'll tell you what I'll do. I'll give you my ID card.

You can keep it if you're not satisfied we've left your sinks cleaner than we find them."

"No." The knife slicing away at the carrots is moving more rapidly. The kitchen crew moves closer.

"Why?"

"Because that's the way I want it."

Then I've had it. It's my twenty-seventh birthday and what am I doing? Confronting some twenty-year-old curly-headed, carrot-slicing schmuck who's getting a charge out of exercising his trivial power?

First the carrot knife goes flying. I go for the curly head, and the guys from Company Aleph take on the kitchen crew. Pots and pans turn into missiles. Dishes are broken. Glasses are shattered. Trays of silverware are spilled. Knives, forks, even spoons are pulled. Guys roll on the floor, crouch under tables. Other guys get locked in storerooms.

Five minutes later, though nobody is seriously hurt, the kitchen is a shambles but the crew from Company Aleph is stacking its dirty dishes on the shelf beside the kitchen sinks. When I turn on the faucet, the water comes out hot.

October 1987

I'm on my way! Off to an air force base for the best of all possible duty. The job that's considered the king of *chuparim.* The goodie of all goodies—paratroop jump school.

As the truck jounces, I remember a conversation I had in 1981 with Amir, a kibbutznik who was then a paratroop commando. When he heard how I had once made an eighteen-hour flight from Okinawa to San Francisco with stops in Tokyo and Hawaii, he said, "Man, you spent all that time in a plane!"

"What are you talking about?" I said. "You're a paratrooper. You've been in dozens of planes."

"Yeah," he said, "but never for more than an hour." Then he laughed.

"What's so funny?" I wanted to know.

"I was just thinking," he said. "I've made more than fifty trips in airplanes but I've never landed in one once."

Compared with basic and advanced infantry training, this is heaven. What discipline there is, is reasonable and congenial. We eat our food in a dining hall, and the food is good—no more battle rations. And though we still sleep in tents, we now have real beds, in which we are allowed to get a good night's rest. No more sleeping in the cold mud or on rocks. Finally, because paratroop training is so demanding, we do very little guard duty.

Right from the beginning the training is fun, though as with everything in the Army, there is a deadly reality behind it. We are being taught how to make and survive combat jumps from an airplane.

I'm glad it's something so serious because on my last leave I was smitten by Ariella. Although Ariella is a real sabra—hot-blooded, good-natured, and direct—she grew up in Tel Aviv, so she's a little more cosmopolitan than the other kibbutznikim. She's also spent several years in Europe with her diplomat parents, which gives her an even broader perspective—and fluency in four languages.

She works in one of the kibbutz day-care centers, which happens to adjoin my own room. Though she moved to the kibbutz some time ago, we didn't much notice each other—until now. Last weekend I finally got up the nerve to introduce myself to the woman who's been soothing the squalling kids next door. It turns out that she's been wanting to find out more about the American soldier who comes home every couple of weeks to go to sleep. We spent hours talking. It also turns out she's intelligent, sensitive, affectionate, and vibrant. And she is the most olive-skinned and almond-eyed woman I have ever met. It will take a lot to keep my mind on my work.

A lot is what I get.

We are divided into classes of twelve and introduced to our instructor. Ya'akov is a short, tanned reservist, who in real life, is a shoe salesman. Here, he is a Master Parachutist and a paratroop instructor. We call him 'sir.'

He marches us out to the training grounds, where we will spend two weeks practicing before we actually jump. Like an enormous playground, the grounds are dotted with huge fake planes, metal towers in a variety of shapes that look like surrealistic jungle gyms, and sandboxes designed for the children of giants. As Ya'akov describes our training schedule, he has to shout to be heard above the roar of the F-15 Eagles and F-16 Falcons taking off on both sides of us. When the larger, heavier F-4 Phantoms roar into the air, he just stops talking.

We get our first lesson in one of the sandboxes.

"Roll," says Ya'akov.

And that's how it all begins. By learning how to roll. The sand is hot; not as hot as the desert, but hot enough. We roll all morning and we roll all afternoon. Rolling to the left, rolling to the right, rolling forward. Tuck in your head, draw up your knees, and roll. Then we are promoted. We get to jump from three-foot-high platforms and roll. We take running jumps and roll. Never mind the sand that gets into our ears and mouth. Roll.

Then the training takes on real dimension as we begin to jump from a variety of towers. One of them reels a soldier out the way a fisherman plays a fish. At the top of another tower I grasp a cross bar, assume a crouching position, and jump, traveling down a length of cable. At a moment chosen by the instructor, I'll be released to fall free. As I hit the ground, I'm supposed to roll.

One of the training towers is so hard on the trainees it's called, in slang, the Eichmann. I climb up to it wearing a fake parachute that straps under my legs and arms the way a real one does. Then I stand at the edge of the tower, waiting for the signal to jump. When Ya'akov yells "Go," I jump, and the Eichmann does its thing to me. Because I've just jumped from a tower that's twenty feet high, I'm set for a certain amount of free fall. But no, I fall only about ten feet, and am yanked to a cruel stop. As I dangle there, I feel a burning sensation on the sides of my neck, my face, and my ears where the parachute ropes have seared my skin. I feel insulted, abused, injured, and that's when Ya'akov pulls another lever that sends me into the free fall I was denied. When I hit the ground ten feet below, once again I roll.

Tommy approaches the Eichmann as a personal challenge. When he hears the command *"Kfotz!* Jump!" he flings himself full force off the tower and into the air like a Hebraic kamikaze. He yells out a four-second count, *"Esrim ve'ehad, esrim ve'shtaim* . . . Twenty-one, twenty-two . . ." but he's cut off by the cable's jolt. What comes out is "Twenty-one, twenty-AAAAAGH . . ."

Repeated jumps from the Eichmann leave a paratroop trainee with burn scars along his neck that give him a certain amount of prestige in Israel, where everyone knows what they mean. When I hitchhike to the kibbutz on weekends, the people who pick me up, seeing the burn marks, say respectfully, "Oh. Paratroop training, eh?!" I am supposed to think of the burn marks as a badge of honor.

There is another tower that simulates jump conditions very realistically. The top of this one is like an airplane and we wait in it hooked up to a cable the way we will be in a real jump. We sit in the semidark waiting to pass through a door on the other side of which there is a sheer sixty-foot drop.

"This is crazy," I think. "Some guy is going to open that door, and he's going to tell me to jump. I've got to be out of my mind."

Then some instructor does just what I knew he would. He shouts, "Platoon, on your feet." "Platoon, check your gear." "Platoon, check the gear of the man in front." Then the door opens and the first thing I notice from this height is that I can't see the horizon. We hook our fake parachutes to the real cable overhead, then each of us follows the guy in front of him as the line moves toward the open door that looks out on the sixty-foot drop.

Suddenly I'm in the air. Actually jumping. I fall for about ten feet and am brought to a jerking halt that is easier than the Eichmann but still simulates the jolt of an opening parachute. If I were wearing a real chute and had jumped out of a real plane, the Velcro bindings of my chute would have been torn open by the static line from the plane well before this moment. I float as I would if held up by my parachute, then I continue my simulated fall, following the cable that leads me to the ground, where I am supposed to land. And, of course, to roll.

This last tower jump shakes loose a certain number of the guys from the paratroop training program. Everybody is scared some of the time during the course of training. Even early on, there are some guys who panic when they are asked to jump from a three-foot step stool, but generally, peer pressure and an occasional helpful push from an instructor keep them going. But this is the tower that separates out those who just can't bring themselves to go on.

In addition to the tower exercises, we put in a certain number of hours watching films and listening to lectures. The best of the films are about sky divers: groups of jumpers who, while they are still in free fall, form star configurations in the sky. We also get answers to some of our most nerve-racking questions: What to do if the chutes don't open. How to handle the chute when you're about to float into high tension wires. How to set down in an orchard or over water.

How to untangle a chute on your way down. What to do if you're about to collide with one of your buddies in midair.

The answers: If your chute doesn't open, you open your reserve chute. To avoid hitting a high wire, you try to make your body as flat as possible, then cross your arms and hope that you'll slide between, below, or above the wires. If you land in an orchard, you try to accomplish the same thing even as you try to cover your face with your arms to keep from being scratched. If you're about to land in water, the idea is to release yourself from the chute entirely just before you hit so you don't get tangled in it. As for colliding with another guy, the drill is that the two of you are supposed to make a deal: "You go to the right, and I'll go to the left." And hope that you've heard each other.

When one of the guys insists on asking, "What happens if your reserve chute doesn't open?" the instructor replies, "Say the *Shema* and look for a haystack."

After all that, it is reassuring to go on a tour of the parachute packing shed, where we watch young women fold parachutes. We are told that these women frequently make parachute jumps because it helps them understand just how crucial their work is.

After three weeks of rolling and jumping from towers and sitting in simulators, we are pronounced ready to make our first real jump.

We are up at three-thirty in the morning. It's late in the summer and the night is warm. The base, at this hour, is quiet. We are carrying our chutes—real chutes. Then, as we wait for the buses that will take us to the runways, some officer comes by and divides us into jump groups. All of a sudden, to my surprise, I'm with a bunch of guys I don't know. I hardly have time to regret not being with my own group when the buses come.

Out on the tarmac we set out our equipment in the order

in which we are going to jump. For the next twenty minutes, while we wait for the planes to roll up, we check ourselves and each other out.

By now the sky has its first hint of blue. There is a thin red line on the eastern horizon when I hear the rumbling of the first plane. No. Not really hear. Actually, I sense the coming of the plane as a sort of rising tension in me. Then, keeping pace with my own excitement, I hear a rumbling and suddenly there is the smell of diesel fuel everywhere. The volume of the roar increases; the entire tarmac begins to shake and we're awash in the wind of the propellors of the Hercules C-130 that now roars by.

It taxis up to the first group waiting in line. Its after end opens and a ramp lowers. Then two rows of soldiers snake their way into the belly of the plane and disappear. A minute later the ramp is raised and the plane rolls off. A second one rolls up and the process is repeated. The third plane is ours. It stops right in front of us, and its ramp slowly descends. We form our two lines and walk up the ramp in reverse order from the way we're going to jump.

It's dark, like the simulation exercises, but now there are vibrations and noise. And there are lights flashing every-where: gauge lights, warning lights, and of course, a couple of feet ahead of me and to the right, the jump signal lights. Red for "Stand by." Green for "Go."

As we take off, we are enveloped by the engines' roar. All of us lean forward yelling "Hey, hey!" to encourage the plane. Then we're in the air and climbing to our jump height —fifteen hundred feet.

I look at the guys around me. Each man shows his ner-vousness in a different way. One guy is prattling a mile a minute to no one in particular. A few are scanning the walls and floors for anything to keep their minds off what they are about to do. Here and there guys are bent over little plastic cards like the one my kibbutz brother, Ron, gave me. Their lips move as they read the *Tfilat Haderech,* the "Prayer for a Journey," which begins:

> May it be your will O Lord our God and God of our fathers to guide us and to direct our steps in peace; to sustain us in peace and to lead us to our desired destiny in joy and peace and to bring us back home in peace . . .

We're all of us packed tight on two pairs of facing benches. We sit shoulder to shoulder, with each guy's knees squeezed between the knees of the guy across from him. Waiting.

The plane is going to make a test pass over the jump site to check wind direction, then it will disgorge us in a series of passes. I'll be number two jumper in the second pass. I think, "Maybe the wind's too strong. Maybe there's a storm out there and they're going to cancel the jump." As the plane makes its first circle, I hear a great "thunk" and the rear door slides open.

First, there's an explosion of white sunlight. Then as my eyes focus, I see how beautiful it is out there. We're over a beach, and I can see the blue ocean and the golden sand. I see the patterns of green and brown the cultivated fields make down below. And I breathe fresh air.

The plane completes its test pass and starts around for the first jump. Some instructor I've never seen before says, "We're going to do it. Group one, on your feet." The plane banks, the warning light turns from red to green, then I hear the lieutenant yell, *"Kfotz, kfotz, kfotz,* jump, jump, jump!!" And one by one all those guys jump out of the plane.

It's crazy. My God, we're fifteen hundred feet above the ground, not sixty feet the way we were in the towers. And those guys just disappeared. They're gone. They're not there anymore.

The plane circles for its next pass. The lieutenant yells,

"Group number two, on your feet." We jump up and, in a kind of shuffle, move toward the light-framed door. Each of us has one hand on a safety strap and the other on the shoulder of the guy in front.

"Count off," the lieutenant shouts.

From behind me and moving forward come the calls, "*Shtem-esrai, beseder,* twelve, OK, *achad-esrai, beseder,* eleven, OK . . ." all the way down till finally the guy behind me taps my shoulder and says, "*Shalosh, beseder,* three, OK," and I yell out, "*Shtaim, beseder,* two OK" as I tap the number one jumper, who yells, "*Achad, beseder,* one OK."

The plane wheels over the jump site. I watch the red "Stand by" light. As soon as the green light goes on, it will be the pilot telling us that we're in the right position. I watch the scenery; I watch the light; I watch the guy in front of me; I watch the instructor. I watch the light.

The green light is on.

The guy in front of me, who is already in position, has only a split second to think about what he's doing, then the instructor slaps him on the back and shouts, "*Kfotz.*" I feel that blow in my heart and the guy is gone. Disappeared.

I get into position just as I've been trained to do. I grab the doorway with both hands. I look down to make sure that half of my foot is in fact hanging over the edge of doorway. It is. The instructor slaps me on the shoulder as he yells, "*Kfotz!*"

I can feel that I'm doing it right. I push myself as far out and as hard as I can, kicking in the direction of the plane's flight, and feel a burst of wind from the prop wash. Sunlight floods my eyes.

Out in the air, I lower my head so that the straps won't tangle me up. I push my body down to make the chute open behind me. And then . . . I lose all orientation.

In order to know what you're looking at, you have to have some reference point. And now, all of a sudden, I haven't got one. I look down and see an airplane flying upside down. I look up and there's the ground twisting round and round. I look to the side and see a guy standing on his head with all kinds of strange straps dangling from him. Nothing makes any sense at all. I know that all the blood in my body has been drained away and replaced with adrenalin. I'm falling. I don't know where I am. Why I am.

I fall and fall. Then all of a sudden, I feel a yank under my arms and under my legs. I look up and see a beautiful green canopy. A green force holding me up in the sky; a power that enables me to fly. The canopy has the shape of the night sky. And slowly the adrenalin drains away and there is blood in my veins again. Looking up, I see the plane above me. It's flying away from me, and there are stick figures spewing from it trailing long strings that suddenly turn into green billows that turn into green canopies that, as I watch, fill the sky.

Green. Green. Green mushroom shapes floating toward the ground. Then I hear a yell. And another yell. "Yay! Whoa! Hey!" Other guys in their opened chutes coming down all around me. Exuberant. Shouting. "I'm alive. Yippee. I did it."

Meanwhile, the ground is rushing up at me. The entire jump, from the minute I leave the plane to when I'm supposed to hit the ground, will last fifty seconds. And it's when one hits the ground that one can get hurt.

We've been told not to look down. "Keep your eyes on the horizon" is the advice. But the ground exerts a pull. It's fascinating to see how small things grow larger as I fall. There's a road down there. A two-lane road. And danger rushing up at me.

I get into my landing position. I reach up and grab the straps and put my feet firmly together just as I have been trained to do, and it turns out to be easy to control my forward motion. I'm moving at just the right forty-five-degree angle when I touch down, hitting the ground almost without impact. Then my chute collapses and it hardly drags me at all.

I look up to make sure that I'm not tangled in my lines; that there's no other jumper about to land on me. With my chute spread out behind me, I prop my helmet under my head and just lie there for a moment looking up, watching the plane making its third pass, spilling another green array of soldiers into the sky. I hear their whoops and yells and feel the warm sand, gritty, like the sand I've been rolling in all week, but peaceful now and fragrant with the smells of the sea and the sage growing on the dunes.

Finally, I have to get up. As I roll up my chute, I become aware of other guys around me rolling up theirs. When we catch each other's eyes, we find we can't stop grinning. These are guys I've never seen before, but there we are rolling up our chutes on a seashore, all of us with the silliest grins on our faces. Because we have all fallen out of the sky and we're alive. We did it. And it feels great.

The very next day, we do a demonstration jump to which parents and friends are invited. They bring with them all sorts of good things to eat at the celebratory picnic that will take place after the jump. We do the jump in great form and then gather near the jump zone waiting to board buses to take us to the site of the picnic.

A snag develops. The parachute school staff and our own 50th Brigade officers, it turns out, have been feuding. The school staff says we haven't been well behaved—that our living area is a mess, and that we've been late for lessons. They decide to cancel the picnic. All of us who have completed our jump have been loaded into buses that are meant to take us to where parents and relatives, who have come from all over Israel and who are loaded down with good things for us to eat, are waiting. But the bus drivers have

been ordered to drive right by the parents and take us all
back to the base.

Of course we are mad as hell, and as the first bus nears
the assembled relatives, some of us shout out the windows,
"Hey, the *mamzerim,* the bastard high brass, have canceled
the picnic. They won't let us stop."

There is a surge of bodies as parents, relatives, and
friends surround the lead bus in which I am riding and
prevent it from moving. People bang on its sides and beat at
its windows. The bus driver turns to the single officer on the
bus and says, *"Nu?* Well?"

"Drive on! Drive on!" the officer shouts, but the banging
gets louder and the shouting more furious. The civilian
driver, seeing that his bus is about to be trashed, says, "Oh,
to hell with it," and opens the doors, front and back.

At first nobody moves. The officer is blocking the front
door and the guy standing in the back stairwell is indecisive.
Although the parents are yelling, urging him off the bus, two
years of army discipline and the stern glare of the officer
keep him from moving.

Finally somebody shouts, *"Kfotz!"* The guy standing in
the rear stairwell responds reflexively and does what he has
been doing for the last couple of weeks. He goes into proper
jump position and at the next *"Kfotz"* launches himself out
into the sea of parents and well-wishers. In less than two
minutes, every one else on the bus has followed his example
and has jumped into the jubilant mob, which then flows
toward the picnic ground.

We have hardly digested the picnic cookies and felafel when
we are required to do a night jump.

Jumping from a plane at night has its own beauty. Waiting
on the tarmac for the plane to come has a more muted feel to
it. When they arrive, the planes seem to loom out of water,
like huge sharks. Indeed, the whole of night jumping has a

kind of underwater quality, as if everything you do is taking place in dark, dark water. When you jump, there is no sudden flash of light; instead you feel as if you are jumping into a vast nothingness, not space, not air. Just nothing. You leap from an environment in which all your senses are on the alert into one in which there are almost no sensual stimuli. You fall in the dark, and though you may see lights, they are subtly indistinct. You can't be sure whether you are seeing the lights of a city or the stars.

And the sea, when you jump over it at night, is an expanse of inky blackness that feels as quiet as you do. The guys coming down in their chutes around you look like emerald ghosts. Even their whoops and hollers have a gentler pitch.

We make our last training jumps in full battle gear. This, after all, is what we're training for. In modern combat, parachute jumps are a bit of an anachronism. Today's large transport helicopters, like the Bell 212 and the Sikorsky CH53, can put troops where they have to be with more precision and safety than a parachute jump. And, in fact, no jump has been made by Israeli army troops in combat since 1956 at the Mitla Pass in the Sinai Desert.

But the training goes on because it's especially demanding and who knows when paratroopers may be needed again.

The jump preparation and the jump scenarios are the same, but loaded down with the weapons bag, we feel as if we are going through them in slow motion. The weapons bag is a canvas sack that holds your rifle, ammunition belt, magazines, canteen, and helmet (total weight: 22 pounds). In addition, we carry whatever equipment the company will require: field radios (weight: 30 pounds), RPGs, rocket-propelled grenades (weight: 20 pounds), and the .50 caliber machine guns. These are enormous weapons. The barrel alone weighs 22 pounds; the gun body about 40. It's such a

big damn gun that its parts have to be divided up between
jumpers.

I jump with the weapons bag strapped to my leg. A line
leads from it to rings hooked into the parachute straps—this
is to keep the weight of the bag from tearing my body in two
at the moment of impact when the chute opens. As I approach the ground, I release part of my reserve chute and let
it move out of the way. Then I trigger the safety clips that
control the strap to which the load is attached. That done, I
watch the weapons bag fall away fifteen feet below me. If all
goes well, it will land a second or two before I do. And all of
this, with time out for enjoying the view, will happen in less
than the minute it takes from when I jump to when I hit the
ground.

No part of army training is absolutely safe, but parachute
training is especially risky. In our platoon alone, we've lost
one guy on the towers (a broken hand) and five more on the
jumps (two have twisted their ankles, two jarred their spines,
and one tore a ligament in his leg).

After our final jump, we get our jump book and our wings.
Then we march to Jerusalem to get our red berets. When
that celebration is over, I'm off to be trained as a squad
commander.

October 1987

Being chosen for squad commander training is not a distinction. Everybody gets a crack at it because the theory is that
you never know who may have to lead a squad.

Once again, we cover the technical aspects of all the
pakalim. This time, though, we don't speciaiize. Each of us
has to know every weapon and tool the squad carries. We go
on exercises in the course of which we rotate *pakalim* to get
hands-on experience with them all. One night, I am a sniper,
the next night a MAGist, and on the third, I may be the
leader of the operation.

We are also given instruction in military theory: strategy, tactics, and even the psychology of leadership. The part of the instruction I like best is navigation. This involves learning how to read aerial maps, air photos, and especially, topographic maps. I learn how every squiggly line or curve on a map represents a change in contour or position of real places.

Once the map is mastered and we know what the terrain we are headed for is supposed to look like, we go on exercise after exercise to plot, memorize, then follow a course.

We're paired for these exercises, which usually take place at night. Each pair is assigned, say, half a dozen mapped targets—wells, caves, houses—spread over a six- or ten-mile area. We plot our course, measuring distances in numbers of strides, and study key details: Half a mile along this stream bed at azimuth 120 degrees a wadi meets the stream bed at 216 degrees. Follow that for 116 double strides (154 yards) till you come to a well. That's target number one.

The details are then memorized, so the enemy won't get any documentation in case we are captured, and we head out into the dark.

Dear Ariella,
It's impossible. I can't see you on Saturdays and still be expected to return to the Army on Sundays.

Yet, here I am. It's another Sunday night, and once again, I'm going nuts.

The whole company is squeezed onto a single truck with all our equipment, presumably waiting to go on a night navigation exercise. I'm still not over being wrenched out of my warm bed at 4:30 A.M. I keep sleeping at intervals: in Haifa, on the bus to Jerusalem, waiting for the truck to take us back to the base, on the truck, right down to just a few minutes ago when I was expected to learn the path for tonight's exercise.

I'm finally awake and ready to go but I'm not quite sure to where. Apparently, everyone else is as confused as I am, though we were given maps to study over the weekend. Of course we studied them, right?

Actually, I like navigation. You go off to a place you've never been, in the middle of nowhere, in the middle of the night. At the same time, if you've studied your map, you really know exactly where you are and where you're going.

And here, where we are, the night exercises take place in rather wonderful places. In terrain, inhabited or not, that has history going back for thousands of years. I like walking by moonlight past a solitary watering well in a deserted valley, or the ruins of a nine-teenth-century village. I'd much rather see it all as a civilian and with you, but for army duty, it isn't bad.

I like the leadership training. All of a sudden, from being one of the guys on a march or an exercise who has nothing to think about except where to put his feet, I turn into the guy who has to lead the men behind me.

On my most successful exercise, I have to lead my squad on a night mission to take three fortified positions on top of a hill ten miles from our starting point. I commit the map of the terrain to memory. Then I identify our objectives and plot a militarily sensible approach to them. I assign a task to each of the ten guys in my squad. Mario will be on the radio; Shakhar will handle the MAG. Finally, before actually setting out, I design the manner of our attack and lead the guys through several practice runs.

I choose a three-pronged approach. One group will position itself at point A to provide cover fire. The rest of us will circle around to attack B. There, we will leave a couple of guys to provide secondary cover fire while the rest of us attack C, our third objective.

When we actually go into action, the exercise is a breeze. The good guys, led, of course, by me, win.

From time to time, we also participate in larger exercises which last as long as a week. On one such excercise we participate in a mock battle to take the Golan Heights. The entire Northern Command is involved, including the Air Force and artillery and tank brigades. At one point, we infantrymen are delighted to find ourselves being transported by helicopter. At another, we work in conjunction with an engineers battalion that moves in with its bulldozers to create huge antitank trenches. They throw up bridges over which our tanks' cross. We follow the tanks on search and destroy missions as they seek out "enemy" tanks, and we move in after them in mopping-up actions.

It's exciting to be part of such a complex action. We infantrymen feel ourselves moving forward and upward, part of an inexorable process which ends when we hear the radio announcement that we've won. We've taken the Golan Heights.

December 4, 1987

Dear Mom and Dad,

I guess it's time for my seasonal letter. The big news! Forty days left before I get out of the Army. Oh, I can taste it. Just thinking of beds and ceilings and coffee with milk and movies and a host of other things that have come to represent civilian life set my skin to tingling.

Strangely, there are some things that I'll miss. Being outdoors, the hard physical work, the excitement. But I figure I can find some of those things in civilian life, too, without the crap that goes with them here. Just being able to make decisions again! Wow!

More, soon.
Love, A.

As we come to the end of squad leaders training, the word comes down that we're being assigned to border patrol. Most likely we're going to be based on the West Bank. It's December and there are no Palestinian or Israeli historical anniversaries to stir up the Arab population. No Fatah Day, no Land Day, no Sixth of June to mark the Israeli presence on the West Bank.

What we hear is that our three weeks there will be easy duty.

10

November 26, 1987

Again kids are getting killed. Damn Army. Yeah, no one ever says it. Damn Army. Six are killed by a terrorist who came out of the sky on a hang-glider. Every one says, "Damn Arabs. Bastard Arabs." And another soldier killed the same day. Damn Arabs. No. His friends killed him by accident. Oh. Swallow it. Where does the anger go? Where can it go?

An exquisite Judean sunset. Thoughts start to drift. My hand reaches out for yours but it's not there.

Left, right, left, right. It's the honor guard practicing for tomorrow's funerals.

Tomorrow. Quick, call the folks. Quick, make the arrangements. Quick, plant the bodies. Quick, before anyone figures out what happened. Figures out who's really to blame.

Can I go to the *brit*, the circumcision feast, tomorrow? A *simcha,* a celebration. A healthy baby boy. Can I go? No. The base is short-handed. Too many funerals. Sorry.

Damn. Damn Army.

And off to Jenin for riot control. Damn Arabs.

Note to myself the day after six Nahal soldiers were killed by a terrorist and a seventh killed by "friendly fire" on a mission in South Lebanon.

December 7, 1987

We've been in Ramallah a week. I room with Tommy and Shakhar in an old hotel and we set about making our room homey. Tommy arranges a "coffee corner," where we keep a heating coil for boiling water, a jar of Nescafé, and some spoons and cups. Shakhar clips photographs of pretty women out of the weekly fashion magazines that we are sometimes given and hangs them above his bed. I make a niche for the letters I've had from Ariella.

Here on patrols, we get the chance to use the skills we've been learning in squad leader's course. A few of us have been made acting sergeants.

Occasionally, I'm in charge of a three-man team doing jeep patrols of the region. Nine hours a day we're out on the road riding through a biblical, pastoral countryside or moving through villages that consist of no more than ten or twelve houses, a general store, and a mosque. Now, in the rainy season, the hillsides and the valleys have turned green. Every brook, stream, and river is swollen and racing. I like it when we find ourselves out of radio range of the base and we go "patrolling" off-road along those streams and over hidden paths.

One of the soldiers sits in the backseat. I sit in front beside my driver, a reservist who, in civilian life, is a very rich man, a toy manufacturer. Now, as we bump along over a

dirt track in the Judaean hills, I remember how he arrived at
the base for his tour of duty, driven there in his shiny black
Volvo by his own driver.

Some days, our job is to ride the Egged buses that go to
the Jewish settlements and the Arab villages in the area. The
buses have lately been a prime target for rock throwers. To
discourage them, two soldiers are on each bus. One guy rides
in front while the guy with the radio rides in back so he can
call for help if it is needed. Our orders: if somebody throws a
rock or a Molotov cocktail, the bus is supposed to stop and
we give chase.

For an infantryman, riding in a vehicle, whether jeeps or
buses, is good duty. And so we settle into a routine which we
expect to maintain for the final three weeks of our service
cycle.

Then, things start to heat up. There are several reasons
for it. First, there is the natural backlog of frustration and
resentment that comes from living under occupation for
twenty years. Paradoxically, this close contact with Israelis
and their values—especially an impatience with established
authority—has contributed to the tension. When the first of
the protestors was arrested, some of the parents excused
themselves: "Look, we tried to keep them at home. We just
can't." The implication was that it was partly the fault of the
Israelis for having introduced Western permissiveness into
their culture.

Then, in November, the Arab League had its summit
meeting in Amman, where the Palestinian issue wasn't even
raised. That silence was seen by the Palestinians as a signal
that they had only themselves to depend on.

But if there was one single event that set the stage for the
surge of protests, it was the hang-glider terrorist attack on
the Nahal central command in late November. In that action,
a single terrorist landed his light aircraft near the base. Then

he shot his way in, killing six soldiers and wounding twenty others before he was killed.

The terrorist's exploit was seen by the Palestinians as a major victory. The image of the invincible Israeli soldier was shattered. A lone Palestinian had gone singlehandedly into an army base and taken on the entire Israeli Army. If he could do that, the least one could do was to throw a rock at a jeep.

What finally ignited what came to be called the *intifada* was a series of events in Gaza. On December 6, an Israeli was stabbed to death in Palestine Square. Two days later, an Israeli semitrailer smashed into two vans carrying Palestinian workers, killing four people. The rumor spread through Gaza that this had been an act of retaliation.

And then all hell broke loose.

December 15, 1987

Dear Ariella,
Tonight's the first night of Hanukkah and here things stink. I'm sure you're hearing about us in the news. I hear it's even being brought up in the UN. Well, it's all that you hear and worse. We've got rocks, tires, all the crap going everyday in the refugee camps. I hate this shit. This time it's not little kids—entire camps are igniting.

Out of the mess certain images stay with me. A girl running home, lunchbox in hand, hugging the walls, eyes filled with tears (from fear? burning tires? gas grenades?). The wild animal eyes of a respectable teacher getting beaten, kicked, and clubbed by six border police for asking why he had to clean up the street clutter—he was only passing through. The broken pride and smouldering hate so apparent in the same guy's down-turned eyes later as he finishes the job. The screams of bewilderment of a mother as we take her son away. The same screams amplified fifty times as she and her friends follow us through the camp finally to be turned away with billy clubs.

I feel weak. Not militarily—I fire the gas and rubber bullets when I have to. I chase and catch with the rest and I know I would shoot without hesitation if I felt it was necessary. The problem is I don't feel that it is. All I feel is shame—human shame for how we're treating other human beings, national shame for forgetting all the lessons of our own history and emulating the worst of our enemies, but mostly personal shame—at my inability to do anything about it. Oh, there are little things we can do, and some of us do them—untying a prisoner's hands so he's a little less uncomfortable. Arranging a deal with UN officials that might ease the confrontations in one camp . . .

It looks like I won't be out until next Tuesday—if then. I'll see you when I can.

Love, A.

The rioting gives no sign of letting up. In village after village, Palestinian flags are raised, barricades are built across roads, tires are burned. Rocks and Molotov cocktails are thrown. In the refugee camps, instead of riots once a week, they come now two or three times a day. And they are no longer spontaneous demonstrations. A local leadership in the towns and villages and in the refugee camps is emerging which designs and orchestrates the protests. Every town, every village is rioting. Ramallah itself has three refugee camps and is surrounded by some twenty villages.

We are kept busy.

We return from patrol to find a bag of candy on every bed. The note inside reads:

Dear Soldier,
Please accept this modest gift as an expression of the nation's identification with her soldiers who, in these times, do their duty in Judea, Samaria, and the Gaza strip in the interests of the security of the state and peace for her citizens.
With feelings of affection and appreciation.

Manpower Branch
The Organization for Soldiers' Welfare in Israel

We are called to Al Amari, where the pattern is typical. Our lookouts on the rooftops watch as the twenty-year-olds sit around over coffee or Coke talking among themselves. Then they call some little kids over and the next thing you know the kids are burning tires near the camp entrance. Meanwhile, people from all over the camp converge toward that spot. Their goal initially is to disrupt traffic on the road outside the gate. Our lookouts call for a patrol and we start off.

By the time we get to the camp gate, several more tires are burning and half a dozen Palestinian flags have been raised. There's a crowd of maybe a hundred people now. The catcalls begin. Taunts about our manhood. Anti-Jewish insults. Graphic descriptions of what they will do to our sisters.

Thick, acrid smoke rises from the burning tires, making our eyes sting. The Palestinians have kefiyahs or handkerchiefs over their faces. The older ones, in their late teens, urge the little kids forward. Rocks aimed at passing cars are now aimed at us, first from a safe distance, then from twenty

yards away. And they're not throwing pebbles. Rocks . . .
I mean baseball-sized rocks.

Twelve of us are standing there. By now, there are a hundred and fifty of them. We're wearing our red berets, not
helmets, because helmets would weigh us down. The barrage
of rocks keeps coming. Some of the Palestinians use leather
slings for their rocks, others fire metal pellets from rubber
slingshots. For the time being we wait.

The jeering crowd advances, throws its rocks, and re-
treats. Then the next wave does the same thing. The smoke
of the burning tires mounts to the sky. The rocks and the
insults fly. Any minute now, we will stop being inanimate
targets. We adjust our billy clubs. We put rubber bullet cannisters on our guns and make sure that we've got blanks in
the chamber with which to fire them.

The third wave comes charging at us. At a signal we run
at them full speed, jumping over the barricade and through
the smoke to meet them. As we run, we try to keep our eyes
on the horizon so we can see the rocks coming at us. I run
and dodge. Gil is running with me. There is the sound of our
gunfire as the rubber bullets do their work. There are
shouts, there are screams, and the crowd of stone throwers
melts. It's like watching water flowing through cracks.
They're just gone.

Gil and I are running through the narrow streets. There's
a particular stone thrower with a ragged sweater we want,
who just hurt Yokhai. The faster we run, the deeper into the
camp we get, and the more dangerous it becomes. Women
hanging out the wash signal which way we're coming. We
could run straight into a dead end and find ourselves surrounded, facing an angry crowd.

We chase our culprit, who we think has run down this
particular street. We try to keep alert because we never know
where the next barrage of rocks will come from. Stuff can be
thrown at you from every side. And not only rocks. Whole

cinderblocks from rooftops; bottles and Molotov cocktails; balloons filled with gasoline. In another unit, guys had such balloons thrown at them followed by burning rags. One guy was badly burned.

"Left," Gil shouts. "He's gone left." So left we go and I catch a glimpse of a ragged sweater disappearing into a corner grocery store and a door slamming behind him.

My heart sinks. I know what it's going to be like. We'll go smashing through the door, and there'll be families inside and the minute they see us the women will start screaming. But the guy's in there.

So, in we go. And sure enough, the store owner and some women see us and the screaming begins.

"Where is he?" Gil asks.

I hear a noise and see what looks like a foot behind the grocery counter. I dash over and reach under the counter and haul the demonstrator up by his sweater. He comes straight up. All the way into the air. He can't weigh more than forty pounds. He's seven or eight years old and he's bawling his heart out. The kid doesn't even have his front teeth.

I put him down and the shame overwhelms me. What am I doing here?

This is the worst work a soldier can do. For eighteen months, I've been trained to deal with people who come at you with guns. I've been taught to react in very clear-cut situations where it's their soldiers on one side and ours on the other. But nobody trained us for this. Where are the Security Guidelines for rubber bullets and eight-year-olds? What are the rules of battle for tear gas and middle-aged women? What have billy clubs got to do with the purity of arms?

The rains continue. My squad stands beside a road flagging down cars so we can check to see if the people in them are on their way to a demonstration. One more ugly task. A car in its own way is like a home, somebody's private territory. Our job, especially on Fridays, when most of the demonstrations in Jerusalem are staged, is to get people out of their cars or taxis and check their IDs. We look for placards on the floor, or PLO flags or leaflets.

And then, when we arrest a guy who's carrying a picture of Arafat and a bunch of propaganda leaflets, he denies everything. "I didn't know what it was. Somebody just gave it to me to give to somebody in my village."

We don't believe him. He doesn't believe it himself. But how is he going to tell us that Arafat is his hero? That he is devoted to the PLO. That the entire West Bank is the PLO.

We're starting to realize that this isn't going to go away anytime soon and neither, probably, are we. We were scheduled to finish this cycle of our army duty at the beginning of January and move on. The sabras are due for *shalat,* their six-month period of agricultural training on a kibbutz. And I'm due to get out, period. But the rumors have it that we'll be here longer than any of us planned, and the consequent anxiety just intensifies our frustrations.

The work is getting to us. The taunts, the screams, the clamoring hatred. Our initial disorientation and shame gives way to anger of our own. We're mad at the Palestinians for throwing their rocks, for swearing at us. For making us arrest them. We blame them first, but there are plenty of others to blame.

Sometimes I blame the press for fanning the flames. They're everywhere and endlessly looking for film opportunities. They have more patrols than we do. The minute there is the least bit of smoke from a tire, there they are, four, five, sometimes ten teams of photographers.

As soon as they show up, the violence escalates. If a group of us is trying to move quietly around a corner, the NBC crew rushes in with their minicams, alerting the rioters that we're there and guaranteeing an acceleration of the barrage of rocks and bottles.

And all that shows up on TV is a disproportionate airing of the "after" picture: "Brutal Israeli military machine in action against poor innocent and unarmed Palestinians." What you rarely see is the "before" picture—the reason the Army was called out in the first place. Families with kids who are bleeding and in shock because a rock has been heaved through their windshield, the glass imploding throughout the car like shrapnel from a hand grenade. Or the burn victims being taken away after fire bombs have turned the bus they were riding into an inferno. Or the soldiers themselves and the wounds inflicted on them in this sticks-and-stones war.

At first, we were given strict orders not to interfere with the media. Israel, after all, is a democracy and has a free press. But as things have gotten worse, the press has been more restricted and I can understand why.

Sometimes I blame the settlers. I have the same mixed feelings about them that I had when I guarded their settlement on Rosh Hashanah last year. If it weren't for these settlements, we wouldn't have to be out here protecting the roads that lead to them. We wouldn't be here at all. The Palestinians could have their damn demonstrations, and we could just stay away.

After that rush of bitterness comes the "on the other hand." Why shouldn't they be allowed to settle where they like? Jews have always been here. What right does anyone have to say this is a land where no Jews are allowed?

On a day-to-day basis, the religious settlers are very good to us. Any hitchhiking soldier seeing four religious Jews in a car that holds five people can confidently expect the car to stop for him—something the secular Jews don't always do. And the settlers are helpful in other ways, too. They organize patrols of their own that search us out in all sorts of weather carrying huge thermoses of hot coffee and hampers filled with cake so we can have a hot drink and a snack while we're out on duty. At Hanukkah time they bring their kids to our base to light candles and sing Hanukkah songs as they try to put some glow into our lives.

December 23, 1987

Dear Ariella,

AAAARGH!! Here I was this morning, in dress uniform, after having my leave postponed three times since last Friday, on my way out the door.

"Where to?" asked the master sergeant.

"Home," I said, my smile spreading from ear to ear, already feeling your hug around me.

"No way," he said.

"He's joking," I said to myself. "He knows how badly I want to go, and he's playing with me."

But no. He wasn't joking. Thursday, it seems, is "Preparedness Day" and we all have to be here.

I don't care. Not about "Preparedness Day"; not about what President Reagan says; not about UN resolutions. I WANT TO GO HOME.

So who knows? Maybe, just maybe I'll see you on Friday, but don't count on me till the twentieth of January. I'm supposed to be out of the Army by then. I hope. . . .

One of the reasons so many people have been killed is simply because we're neither trained nor equipped to deal with situations like these. We're combat soldiers trained for combat.

Our orders are clear and meant to be fair: we're not to fire unless our lives are threatened. But I think we

would feel a lot less threatened if we had been trained
in riot control and had better riot gear.

In case you're starting to think that I've joined the
intifada and am about to start wearing a kefiyah and
throwing stones at the soldiers—don't. One of the
things we're responsible for—along with Shin Bet
agents—is arresting terror suspects. When we go after
guys who've committed real crimes, I have no problem
being part of the arrest. Even if it's rough.

Later: Hey! The news is suddenly good. It now looks
as if I'll be able to see you tomorrow after all. So I'll be
able to give you this letter—after I've hugged you for
about ten minutes.

I miss you, but I'll see you soon.
Love, A.

One of the things our training lacks is a course in Arabic.
When a crowd of men and women surges screaming toward
us and we don't know what they're saying, the violence is
likely to escalate. In fact they may only be crying, "Please
God, at least tell me where my son is."

As it is, we only know how to say, "Open the door."
"Open your trunk." "Let me see your ID card." And both
sides have a pretty extensive vocabulary of each other's
swear words.

Three of our guys in a jeep are on patrol near a refugee
camp when the engine dies. They have trouble raising the
base on their radios so two of them decide to go to higher
ground where there will be less interference. Like idiots,
they leave the driver alone in the jeep. While they're gone,
he tries to push-start the jeep and it gets away from him,
rolling downhill. Of course he runs with it trying to stop it,
but it just keeps going until it rolls to a stop inside the
refugee camp. His buddies on the hilltop see what's happening and they radio us for help. By the time we get there,

there is plenty of reason to be nervous. The three guys are standing beside their jeep as a crowd, getting bigger by the minute, forms. It's just a question of time before somebody picks up a rock.

Well, there we are, the reinforcements, standing around, trying to figure out how to get the disabled jeep restarted while keeping a wary eye on the crowd. An old Palestinian comes limping up to me. Pointing to my ammunition belt he says, "There's one of them over there," and he indicates the direction of the hill.

I don't know what he's talking about but I take one of my buddies and follow the old man a hundred yards or so up the hill where a small crowd has gathered around a fully loaded ammunition belt lying in the middle of the road. The belt holds eight magazines of shells, plus tear gas grenades and billy clubs. Clearly it has fallen from the disabled jeep and clearly it's somebody's stupid mistake. But the crowd around it sniffs at it as if it were some dangerous animal, fascinated by it, yet afraid to touch it lest the thing has been put there as a trap. The whole charade ends a minute later when I pick up the belt, thank the old man, and go back to our jeep with my friend. By this time, the other jeep has been fixed and we roar out of there, that ridiculous adventure over.

Until things started to get this far out of hand, our guys were split more or less down the middle about how to handle demonstrators. Without official encouragement, there were guys who were rough from the start. Their line was, "It's the only language they understand. What do you think they'd do to you if they had the chance? How did the Syrians treat them? And the Jordanians?"

The rest of us looked at our service on the West Bank as an unpleasant, necessary task, but we saw no need to man-handle the people we arrested. Our line was, "He's caught. He's going to jail. What good will it do to hit him? It just adds to the general level of hatred. Besides, what would you do if you were a Palestinian?"

Early on, the second group restrained the first to some degree. But when the Army realized that this wasn't just a wave of violence, they called in a division commander to direct the overwhelming number of troops here, more now than it took to conquer the West Bank in 1967.

He appoints us his "commandos," and we are sent wherever there is trouble. That now includes every little village in our region. His parting words are, "Violent demonstrations are to be broken with violence."

With that kind of tacit approval, and our own deepening frustration, though we never officially hear about Defense Minister Rabin's "Iron Fist" policy, our impulse to restrain violence is eroding. We soldiers are tired of being the object of daily hatred.

The feeling of revulsion builds up inside. "They," the people with the rocks and the filthy epithets, want to do us bloody damage. We've had concussions, broken collarbones, and more gashes and bruises than we can count. I've had my forehead cut open more than once. When the blood flows, I don't give much of a damn about the motivations of the guy who threw the rock. He's hurting me, and if he could, he'd kill me. Just then it's hard to remember the forty years that led up to this mess, the squalor in the camps or the Palestinians' lack of fundamental rights. Here there is neither history nor politics. There is only action and reaction.

January 4, 1988

Dear Ariella,
Happy New Year . . .

Here, everything stinks and is getting worse. Yesterday, a guy in our company killed a young woman by accident in Al-Ram. We've now lost our CO and the soldier who fired; it's not clear for how long. I'm tired of being here—tired of chasing kids, tired of hearing women scream, tired of dodging rocks, tired of the whole bit . . .

For New Year's Nathan came and spirited Tommy and me away to Jerusalem (the assistant CO gave us a five-hour leave), where we made a serious spaghetti meal. Then back for guard duty on the roof, where we had champagne and fired off flares at midnight. Then back to work. January 1 is Fatah Day . . .

I miss you. Love, A.

Though we don't talk about our feelings much among ourselves, when a reporter from *Ma'ariv* comes to interview us about the violence, it is an occasion to open up.

Dror says, "It's hard on us to use the billy clubs. Sometimes I don't understand how they can ask us to do this."

"We are fed up," Uzi says. "We feel like stretched gum."

"When you are attacked, you think of nothing," Gal says. "Then I strike hard. But at night, when I can think about what happened, it bothers me."

And Uri says, "I once believed in coexistence. Now I'm not sure it's possible. One thing I do know, none of us will ever forget any of this."

Captain Yaron, the assistant regimental commander, is worried: "At first our soldiers did not know how to wield their billy clubs. Now they are used to it. They land their clubs with all their might. The question is, 'Will we be able to take the West Bank out of the troops after they get out of the West Bank?' "

Lieutenant Colonel Israel, the commanding officer of our brigade, tells us, "The worst thing that can happen to you here is losing your human and personal character. I want everyone to understand that there is no black or white. We can't separate ourselves from our thoughts and emotions. A soldier who has doubts is better than one who is inflexible."

We are in something of a double bind. In any war, a soldier gets to use his gun. But in this sticks-and-stones war of ours, though we carry guns, we are continually reminded that we must use them only as an absolute last resort, if our lives are directly threatened. Before we go on patrol, we receive the familiar briefing, "Don't shoot. Don't shoot if you can avoid it. If someone is shooting at you, if you can see the source of the fire, and if it is endangering human life, then you can return the fire. If somebody throws a hand grenade or a Molotov cocktail, you can fire. Otherwise, you damned better be prepared to show your commanding officer (and his commanding officer) that your life really was in danger."

Still, tragic accidents can happen. Ronni, one of our guys, a medic, was chasing a rioter and somehow got separated from his squad. Ronni is a sweet guy who hated having to do service on the West Bank. But there he was, alone and suddenly surrounded by a crowd of hostile villagers. So he fired into the air.

But he made a terrible mistake. Our orders are that before you fire into the air, you must first check your sights. And Ronni didn't do that. The shot he fired struck a woman who was hanging out her laundry.

When Ronni got out of the village, he was immediately arrested, and our company commander was suspended until the incident could be thoroughly investigated.

The general in command of the region dressed us down. "Well, whom have you killed? A woman. And what was she doing? She was hanging out her laundry. So what have you accomplished? You've escalated the violence. Because every time you have a death, you have a funeral, and every time you have a funeral, you have a riot. Emotions build up. You have made another martyr."

Ronni comes from a politically left wing family and has served on the West Bank reluctantly. He has occasionally quarreled with his comrades about their rough treatment of Arabs. Released from prison after an inquiry, Ronni has been moody and withdrawn. He rejects his friends' efforts to cheer him.

In its January 29 edition, *Ma'ariv* gives Ronni's account of the incident.

> Our mission was to capture and arrest rioters in Al-Ram village. I ran after one of the men who was identified as a leader [of the riot]. The two of us reached an alley. He started to attack me. He was a big man who could have thrown me easily. I didn't want to shoot him, so I fired into the air. For a moment, he stopped, stunned, but the people behind him urged him on and he came at me again. The crowd was all around me and I felt myself in danger. Again, I fired into the air.
>
> Then I saw the woman lying there. I didn't know what had happened to her. There was not a drop of blood showing. I'm a medic and I intended to help her, but I was alone in the midst of a rioting crowd and I knew that if I bent down to help her someone would stab me in the back. And I didn't believe they would let me undress her to treat her. So I turned the rioter loose and let him run away while I went to find someone to cover me. When we came back, the woman was gone. Four hours later, our regional commander told me that I had killed her. I was in shock. . . .
>
> It's a nightmare. As time goes by I find it harder and harder to believe that I killed someone who had done me no harm.

One of my fears is that in the course of duty I will run into my Palestinian friend Khalid.

Khalid's family has always treated me with kindly consideration. When I visited his home, his mother, who doesn't

speak English, communicated with smiles and frequent help-
ings of cake and tea. Khalid's father is an administrator for a
UN school in one of the refugee camps. One of Khalid's
sisters studied medicine in Czechoslovakia; his other sisters
have gone to school in the United States and in Romania.

In their home, I did not wear my uniform and the family
seemed able to accept my presence as Khalid's friend. But
sometimes when the events around us intruded and became
the subject of our discussion, the civility with which I was
treated wore a little thin. One day, we were talking about an
Israeli soldier who had been stabbed while doing guard duty
on the West Bank. Khalid's father said, "Well, I understand
the political pressure that produced the stabbing, but as a
human being I feel sorry for the soldier and his family."

Khalid's sister said sharply, "Well, I'm not. I hope he rots
in hell. He had no business being on the West Bank to begin
with." The message to me was clear. So long as I was an
Israeli soldier on the West Bank, I would deserve whatever
happened to me. Meanwhile, in the family living room, I was
Khalid's friend.

Both sides made careful distinctions between who we are
and what we represent. But now, as the uprisings intensify, I
can feel things changing. I am haunted by the thought that
when we were in Nablus, some of the tear gas we fired might
have wafted into their home. And when I have to go on
house-to-house searches, I keep thinking, "This isn't just
some suspect's home. It could be Khalid's."

Sometimes, when we confront demonstrators, I keep a
nervous eye out to see if Khalid is in the crowd. This is
especially true when we are in Ramallah, where Bir Zeit
University is. My nightmare is that we'll get orders that will
send us in to face student demonstrators and that Khalid will
be there.

Then one day, I do run into him.

I am in uniform, with my unit. We have just broken up a

riot and I am standing beside our command car when we spot each other across the street. The moment seems to freeze. We conduct a silent, helpless conversation with our eyes. I say, "My God, things are getting out of control. I'd rather be anywhere than here." And he replies, "Yeah. This is terrible. This shouldn't be happening at all."

Then our dilemma becomes acute. I start to walk toward him even as I think, "No. I can't talk to him. If his friends see him talking to me, they'll decide he's a collaborator. And my friends will wonder just what my relationship with him is." And yet, it is clear we want to say something to each other, so I keep walking and he keeps waiting. When I reach him I say in the most offhand manner, "Hey, you. Let's see your ID." His half-smile is ironic as he hands me his identity card. Under the cover of that exchange, we are able to arrange to meet again later.

In civilian clothes, I go to Nablus to visit Khalid and his family. Because I'm driving a car with yellow (Israeli) license plates, I'm in danger of being stoned. But I've learned a useful trick. I put a kefiyah up on the dashboard. Passing groups of Arabs on the roadside, I flash them a V sign, thereby saving my windshield. When I get to the Israeli checkpoints, I put the kefiyah under my seat, put on my dark Ray Bands, and call out in Hebrew, "Hey guys. How're you doing?" to the men on duty and they wave me right by.

As I drive through the West Bank, the residue of violence is visible on the roads—the rocks, broken glass, and tear-gas cannisters strewn over the asphalt that is occasionally scorched by burned tires. But I realize that the real change is in the faces of the people that I pass.

I catch the alertness in the wide eyes and tense movements of soldiers on foot patrol as they scan rooftops and doorways for the source of the next inevitable attack. What will it be this time? Cinder-blocks? Gas bombs? Maybe a knife in the back?

But it is the faces of a group of young Palestinians as they watch the patrol pass that causes me to pull over. From the protective anonymity of my civilian car, I see the new hatred in each of those faces—it is a sharp, burning hatred so vivid and so palpable that it makes my eyes sting like stale tear gas.

I knew in my mind that things had changed since the *intifada* began, but I didn't really *feel* it until now. I start the engine and drive on.

I arrive in Nablus and go to Khalid's house. I knock at the door and it is opened by his mother, but her face has changed too. Instead of her usual smiles and nods, when she sees me she bursts into tears and, leaving me in the open doorway, goes back into the house to call Khalid. Throughout my visit, I catch glimpses of her in the next room, shaking her head and crying.

January 16, 1988

Dear Ariella,

It snowed last night. Sometimes it just takes a little trigger like that to send me into a reverie of a future where things are, well, normal.

I'll say, "Hey, it's snowing outside. Let's sit on the porch and watch it fall."

"Mmm. Sounds nice. You bring the coffee, I'll get the blankets."

It snowed on and off today but it didn't last. I wish it would. I wish it would just cover the whole area in white and let us start all over again.

I love you,
A.

Epilogue

Finally, on the tenth of February, my discharge papers come through. I'm to report to the induction center on February eighteenth. On the fifteenth, my company is ordered to fold up and head back to our permanent base, where we will sign off on our equipment. We're going home.

It's been a couple of months since I have been an acting sergeant, but it's only now that my time in the Army is up that I am officially issued my stripes. Three days later, I show up at the induction center, where all this started a year and a half ago. This time, I turn in all my uniforms and equipment. I get to keep one pair of shoes, my dog tags, and my POW card for reserve duty and that's it. A year from now and every year after that until I'm fifty-five, I'll be called back for a month of reserve duty.

It will be strange to be out. And bittersweet. On the one hand, I'm happy as hell to go; on the other hand, I'm leaving a lot of my friends behind. Tommy, Mario, Danno, and Manni all have to serve between nine and twelve months more. The sabras are off to their kibbutzim, but they will be back in six months to finish their active service.

I'm going home! And I feel disoriented. For a year and a half, there was always somebody telling me where to go, what to do, how to do it. Now, nobody is telling me anything.

Then there's Ariella. I'm anxious to see her, but I'm also a little nervous. We've never spent more than a weekend together. What's it going to be like on that third day we never had? What will we talk about?

It is nearly ten o'clock when I am finally signed out. The morning is bright and springlike, though the air is still a little crisp. I'm wearing a borrowed civilian jacket because I hadn't realized I would have nothing warm to wear after turning in my uniform. As I empty my pockets, I come upon a soldier's special-fare bus ticket. As I leave the induction center, I pass a newly uniformed soldier still looking awkward and terribly clean in his pressed trousers and green beret. A real *bizbuzz*. I pat him on the back and hand him the bus ticket as I say, "Here, I think you can use this more than I can." Then I'm off to the bus station where, as a civilian, I pay full fare for a ticket to my kibbutz.

About the Author

Aaron Wolf grew up in San Francisco and spent several years in Israel before becoming a citizen in 1985. He has served in the American Merchant Marines and the Israeli Army.

He is currently doing graduate work in water resource management at the University of Wisconsin in Madison.

Book Mark

The text of this book was set in the typeface Bodoni Book
by Berryville Graphics, Berryville, Virginia.

The display was set in Radiant Bold Condensed
by All-American Photolettering, Inc.,
New York, New York.

It was printed on 50 lb paper
and bound by Berryville Graphics, Berryville, Virginia.

DESIGNED BY ANN GOLD